WRITING

TEACHER'S BOOK

WRITING

Teacher's Book

Ron White and Don McGovern

New York   London   Toronto   Sydney   Tokyo   Singapore

PRENTICE HALL INTERNATIONAL ENGLISH LANGUAGE TEACHING

First published 1994 by
Prentice Hall International
Campus 400, Maylands Avenue
Hemel Hempstead
Hertfordshire, HP2 7EZ

A division of
Simon & Schuster International Group

© International Book Distributors Ltd

Typeset in 11/12 Garamond
by Fakenham Photosetting Limited

Printed and bound in Great Britain by
Redwood Books, Trowbridge, Wiltshire

British Library Cataloguing in Publication Data

A catalogue record for this book is available from the British Library

ISBN 0–13–303736–3

2 3 4 5 98 97 96

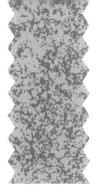

CONTENTS

INTRODUCTION: THEORY AND PRACTICE

During a course in academic writing, students will want to develop the skills appropriate to writing essays for a degree course. We can assume that most of these students will have done some academic writing before, either in their own language or in English. Few of them, however, will have done the kind of extended academic writing in English which they will be required to do as part of a degree course.

CONVENTIONAL METHODOLOGY: DECONSTRUCTING THE TEXT

Academic writing has its own conventional forms, manner of organisation and expression. It is possible, as with all types of discourse, to deconstruct academic writing and to identify specific functions, such as description, classification, narration, generalisation, argument, and so on. It is also possible to deconstruct sections of discourse into thesis, support and conclusion. Characteristic ways of encoding these various discourse functions can be defined and typical ways of linking ideas can be demonstrated.

Having deconstructed the discourse into these elements, it is possible to train students in producing the elements in a controlled or guided fashion with the ultimate intention of combining the elements in the various ways required. Models of the target product can be used to demonstrate what it is that the students should aim to achieve.

Such an approach is representative of many academic writing courses. The limitation of such an approach is that it often focuses on *what* (the product) at the expense of *how* (the process). It is rather like showing an apprentice potter a finished piece of pottery without demonstrating the throwing of the pot on the wheel and the various processes of decorating, glazing and firing which result in the final product.

A NEW APPROACH: FOCUSING ON PROCESS

Although it is helpful to know what the final product looks like, it is also necessary to know how to carry out the processes which make the product possible. This is, in short, the philosophy behind the approach to teaching academic writing which is the basis of this course. It can be summed up in the following diagram:

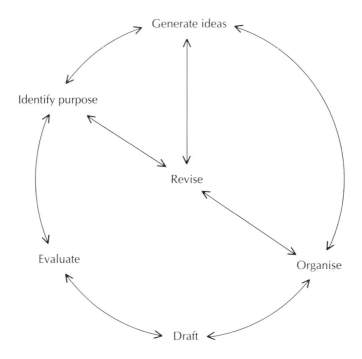

This diagram is intended to emphasise the recursive character of writing. It is not a simple linear process, even though the final product is linear text and even though, in one sense, the process occurs in some kind of linear sequence in real time. What all the research evidence shows (and what, once we think of it, our own experience will confirm) is that writing is an extremely complex thinking process in which, especially in academic writing, there is a great deal of darting to and fro among the various processes, as shown in the diagram.

Likewise, the Writing course is intended to help develop the skills involved in these processes. This means that writing sessions will give priority to composing and that there will be much less emphasis on mimicking a product than is common in most model-based approaches to teaching writing. Obviously, there are conventions which students will have to learn and adhere to. But these conventions – whether of organisation, style or grammar – will have to be seen within the context of producing a piece of writing with an intended purpose and audience. The conventions of academic – or any – writing do not exist for their own sake.

Most conventions exist because they serve the purpose of aiding communication, and members of the discourse community expect that writers will conform to the conventions of that community.

THE 'NORMS OF COMMUNICATION'

What, in short, writers have to consider is what we might call the 'norms of communication'. Whenever we engage in any kind of communication which requires language, we operate within a framework of unspoken rules or conventions. Since these conventions apply just as much to written as to spoken communication, it is important for writers to observe them because their readers expect them to do so. Thus, readers expect that writers will give them neither more nor less information than is needed to understand the message. They assume, too, that writers will not give them information which they know to be false, or for which they lack sufficient evidence, or which is irrelevant to their purpose in writing. And finally, readers expect writers to use language which is clear, unambiguous, concise and straightforward. If writers deliberately flout these unwritten norms, they do so in order to make some kind of extraordinary impact on their readers or because they want to set new trends. If, however, they simply fail to observe these conventions, they run the risk of producing writing which is unsatisfactory and ineffective.

Such failure may arise from not adequately taking the audience into account. This is easily done when writing because, in many ways, writers have to make greater efforts to do this than speakers. Lacking the immediate feedback of an audience, writers have to develop a sense of self-evaluation to make up for lack of reactions from their intended audience. Writers have to try to read what they have written with eyes other than their own, anticipating their readers' reactions and adjusting their writing accordingly. Doing this involves them in a range of evaluative activities: considering, for instance, how much knowledge they share with their readers and how much is exclusive to themselves; or deciding how to 'package' their information to achieve their purpose in writing; or judging whether the language they have chosen conveys the whole of their meaning; or making sure that readers will be able to follow the train of thought that underlies the whole text. Some of this evaluation may be culture-specific with the result that students may have to acquire new conventions.

AWARENESS OF PRODUCT: INPUT

At the same time there is often a need to provide students with appropriate samples of language use in relation to particular functions (e.g. cause/effect, comparison/ contrast) and patterns of organisation so that they have a clear sense of accuracy. If appropriate examples are introduced carefully in authentic contexts and especially at later stages in their composing process – after students have begun to formulate their own ideas – there is usually less risk of these samples being treated as models for rote imitation. For this reason a degree of product 'input' in terms of both linguistic and rhetorical form has been included with a clear and integral relation to each writing task.

Students are frequently referred to Evaluation Checklists A and B on pages 21 and 29 of the Students' Book and to Appendices 1 and 2 on pages 67 and 68. The evaluation checklists help students to monitor input, structure and cohesion in their written drafts. Encourage frequent discussion of points arising from the use of the checklists and ensure that students learn to apply the advice they contain as part of their writing routines.

The appendices are referred to within the evaluation checklists and at other points in the students' instructions.

- **Appendix 1** (page 67) lists cohesive markers under their general type but does not give syntactic contexts for the markers. You will no doubt need to spend some time helping students to:
  – choose appropriate markers for given contexts
  – become familiar with the subtle differences of meaning and syntactic use which distinguish them
  – avoid overuse of these markers in their writing.

- **Appendix 2** (page 68) gives syntactic breakdowns of the uses of comparison and contrast markers, which are particularly complex. These markers are not included in Appendix 1, so remind students to use both appendices for reference purposes.

- **Appendix 3** (page 70) gives guidance on ways of referring to data and statistics in tables and diagrams.

- **Appendix 4** (page 71) suggests several ways of either showing personal commitment to written opinions or avoiding and tempering commitment to them. This is an important and sensitive area of academic writing that students need to learn to control carefully. According to the subject in hand and their sources of information, they will need to adopt a more or less authoritative tone.

- **Appendix 5** (page 72) is a useful resumé of the procedures recommended throughout the course.

The overall aim of this material has been to achieve a practical synthesis of approaches to writing – a process methodology combined with reader-oriented and product approaches to writing. By combining these approaches in a balanced and practical way, we hope to overcome some of the binary opposition – the 'either/or' thinking – which has characterised much of the recent debate on the process/ product issue.

CLASSROOM PROCEDURES

One of the aims of the Writing course is to develop these kinds of awareness in the students. This is essentially a methodological issue, which will be exemplified in the classroom through the use of techniques with which you will already be familiar. These include the use of different combinations of group work and peer collaboration. If students are to develop a sense of audience and a set of criteria which they can eventually apply to their own writing, they need to do this within their own immediate discourse community – their own group or class. Thus, writing sessions will involve brainstorming, discussion, and reading and reacting to each other's writing. The sequence of steps can be summarised as follows:

- discussion (class, small group, pair)
- brainstorming/making lists
- planning/rough writing
- preliminary self-evaluation/peer evaluation
- first draft
- self-evaluation/peer evaluation (teacher evaluation)
- further self-evaluation/editing
- second draft
- evaluation and marking by teacher.

Such a sequence will not be invariable. Some writing will go to a third draft. And not all writing will begin with a discussion. Editing – which is the penultimate tidying up of surface and mechanical features before writing the final draft – will be done at a later stage if the writing goes as far as a third draft. There should be a 'workshop' atmosphere throughout in which students and teachers collaborate, with students taking note of suggestions from their peers and developing a routine of critical thinking and continual improvement of their work.

THE TEACHER'S ROLE

This brings us to your role as teacher. Such an approach to writing depends on your skills as an organiser, facilitator, adviser, respondent and informant. Most of what emerges from each session should come from the students, with you acting as prompt, guide, questioner and organiser. You will need to set up the class in ways which promote collaborative as well as individual work. You will judge when it is appropriate to move from one stage of the activity to another. You will help to direct the class towards productive outcomes. Letting the students ramble around in an undirected and largely fruitless enterprise is not the idea – initially you may need to guard against this assumption on the students' part. And you will need to intervene where appropriate with enabling activities, advice, use of reference books and checklists and, if the students need it, conventional language input.

GIVING PRIORITY TO WRITING

Keep in mind, however, that these are writing classes and not language classes. It is very easy for the writing class to be hijacked so that it becomes yet another lesson on the past perfect or some other grammatical point. Clearly, language cannot be ignored in any writing class in which the students are not native users of English; but concern with language should be in the context of composing. The purpose of the class is to facilitate the best piece of writing possible, given such exigencies as the linguistic and conceptual sophistication of the students, their knowledge of the subject and their ability to produce a piece of discourse which conforms to the 'norms of communication' described earlier. Attention to language correctness should be seen within this context.

So, go for ideas and organisation and coherence first. Then go for language. This means that in the earlier stages of generating, assembling and organising ideas and of producing the first draft, priority should be given to composing skills and the development of the writer's message. It is in the transition from early draft or drafts to final draft – to the finished product – that the focus shifts to language form. This focus may involve dealing with the 'old chestnuts' – subject-verb concord, verb endings, article usage, prepositions, tense usage, etc – as well as with the reconstruction of sentences to make the meaning clearer or the message snappier. Dependent clauses, for instance, provide ways of packaging information with clarity and economy and students may need help in rephrasing redundant or ambiguous sentences as they move from penultimate to final draft. Some guidance may be needed in helping students to use the cohesive markers in the appendices when rephrasing sentences.

Finally, the writing class should be a place where students write – and they should be encouraged to write as much and as fast as possible. Most writing assignments will be from one and a half to three sides of A4 paper in length, depending on the nature of the task and the proficiency of the student. In simple terms, this means that as much as possible of the writing students produce should have a beginning, a middle and an end. They should be writing complete texts rather than isolated sentences, which tends to be what many conventional writing programmes deal with. No matter how short the piece of writing, it should be a complete structure.

Obviously, not all of the students' time will be spent with pen on paper because writing does not begin with the act of transcribing – a point which you may need to make at first. Writing involves thinking, gathering and shaping ideas and making use of readers' reactions, all of which can be done in the classroom. The members of the class (including the teacher) are a community, and by developing a sense of awareness as a discourse community in their class, the students should be enabled to make the transition to becoming members of the particular academic discourse community which they will join on leaving the course.

INTEGRATION WITH THE READING COURSE

The Writing course can either be used on its own or in conjunction with the Reading course in this series. The topics and features of language use covered are linked to those covered in corresponding Reading units, which are intended to precede the Writing units. This means that, having already covered a topic in the Reading book in this series, students should have ideas for content when they tackle the same or a related topic in the Writing book. The Reading units also prepare students to recognise and analyse the various rhetorical functions and patterns of organisation found in academic writing. This becomes a graduated preparation for producing these functions and patterns of organisation in essays in the corresponding Writing units. In other words, the tasks and activities in each pair of integrated Reading and Writing units are all sequenced and structured in such a way as to culminate in the final writing activity.

UNIT 1

WRITING ABOUT WRITING

INTRODUCTION

One of the aims of this unit is to begin to develop a sense of community among a group of people who have never worked together before. One way of doing this is to focus on a common set of experiences and to exchange ideas about them.

Before beginning the essay-writing lesson, explain to the students that in this course they are going to do a lot of writing, because we learn to write by writing. But we also improve our writing by rewriting. So, they will be rewriting as well as writing. Sometimes they will work with other students and at other times by themselves.

They will begin by looking at their own experience of writing. The aim is to:

- get to know about each other's previous experience
- let their reader know about their writing
- analyse their previous writing experience
- have a shared topic to write about.

It is suggested that you go through the section 'Introducing this book' in the Student's Book *after* you have worked on the questionnaire in Task 1. This will give you a more accurate indication of the students' assumptions about academic writing.

TASK 1

Academic writing questionnaire

1.1 Explain that in the activities in this unit the students are to work on an essay. They will work individually and in pairs.

1.2 Lead into the topic in whatever way you feel is appropriate.

1.3 Go over the questionnaire (whether photocopied or in the book) and establish that the students (a) understand the items and (b) understand what to do. Then tell them to complete the questionnaire individually. Allow about 20–30 minutes.

1.4 Emphasise that there are no 'right' or 'wrong' answers to the questions and that the students should be frank about their views. The questionnaire is designed to get them to think about their *individual* experience of academic writing. If some students still seem unsure about how to approach the questionnaire, try to help them into the process by asking similar questions in different terms.

Some students who come from conservative learning cultures may find this exercise rather alien at first, particularly if they have never been asked to think analytically about their academic writing before.

1.5 Organise the class into groups of two, three or four. Tell them to compare their answers to the questionnaire and to make a note of items where they all have similar answers or where there are striking differences.

1.6 In plenary, ask the groups to report the outcome of their group discussion. Ask students to identify common responses to the items as well as different ones. Certain points are likely to be common to most students, whereas others may be unique to one student.

1.7 You may want to refer to current trends in thinking among applied linguists and ELT specialists in relation to questions 1, 2 and 3. Questions 2 and 3 will help to expose some of the preconceptions of those students who think of grammar as being of prime importance to academic writing – many of whom will expect the writing class to be a grammar class. (You may want to counter this expectation at the outset.) Surveys carried out among academic departments in British universities suggest that content, organisation and vocabulary are considered most important by subject tutors in the academic writing of overseas students. Many tutors will tend to overlook minor errors in grammar, as long as they do not seriously interfere with comprehension.

1.8 With regard to question 4, it may be a good idea to elicit the various forms of academic writing which can involve different kinds of communication with a reader. This comunication is not always one-way. For example, replies to academic texts are written in the form of letters, articles, conference papers and so on by people with opposing points of view. You could mention:

- published academic books
- articles published in academic journals
- papers given at academic conferences
- dissertations and unpublished monographs found in libraries
- essays given by students to tutors.

You could then consider the possible forms of communication that could result from each.

1.9 You may want to ask students to suggest headings for each item in the questionnaire. These headings can provide a basis for paragraphs, and a collection of such paragraphs can form the basis of the essay which they will draft, if they intend to draw on the information in the questionnaire.

1.10 Refer again to question 4 in the questionnaire. Emphasise the importance of thinking about the identity of the reader. Point out that a writer should always consider the following:

- Who will my reader(s) be?
- What does my reader already know about the topic?
- What will my reader want to know?
- Why will he or she want to know it?

Task 2

In this task, the students will write their first draft.

First, ask students to summarise what they did in the previous activity. Discuss the points relating to readership. Remind students of the similar points you made at the end of Task 1. You could also ask them to think about the questions they would want to ask their reader if he or she were writing for them on the same topic. This may help to establish the idea that writers and readers are united in a kind of dialogic relationship, even when they have never actually met.

Consider the organisation of the essay. Review the different ways of organising suggested at the beginning of Task 2 in the Student's Book. Either add another of your own or elicit suggestions from the students. Make sure that they understand the different ways of organising ideas indicated in 2.2.

The suggested length for the essays is intended to be flexible. Some students will not manage much more than 300 words at this stage, while others may want to write more than 500. It may be best to set an upper limit of, say, 600 words so that students are aware of the need to be concise and organised in their approach.

 Step 1

2.1 This is the brainstorming stage. Encourage students to be spontaneous in this and not to worry about the order of ideas at this stage. Give them about five minutes to brainstorm, longer if you feel it is necessary. Emphasise that they should use *rough notes* rather than complete sentences. They can use words, mind maps, diagrams or visual images – whatever comes naturally. If some of the wording comes in their first language, tell them not to worry about this. The important thing is to achieve a rapid and spontaneous 'flow' of ideas which can then be developed into a plan. Emphasise too that neatness is not important. Some students may inhibit themselves by thinking at this stage about their presentation and the impression made upon a teacher.

2.2 This is the planning stage. When they seem ready, tell students to go over the notes from their brainstorming and to begin the process of ordering and grouping them. You may want to demonstrate the principle involved by putting up some ideas on the board and grouping, regrouping and numbering them.

Circulate and see if some students have persisted in writing out full sentences instead of using rough notes during their brainstorming. Show them how full sentences can be reduced to note form by focusing on key words. Emphasise how much time this will save. Otherwise they are effectively writing rather than brainstorming and planning. By concentrating on grammar and vocabulary they can be distracted from the immediate purpose. If the problem seems widespread, deal with some examples on the board or overhead projector.

2.3 When they are ready, ask students to exchange plans with a partner and evaluate each other's plans. Circulate and monitor their responses to the suggested questions. Intervene as necessary. Less proficient groups will tend to need careful guidance at this stage.

You may want to postpone the peer evaluation of plans until Unit 2 or 3, especially if the group is less proficient or seems to have initial difficulty in adapting to the 'process' approach. It is also time-consuming to conduct two peer evaluations – on both the plan and the first draft – for the same writing task. Nevertheless, it is suggested that you ask the students to evaluate each other's plans in at least a few of these writing tasks. The time spent on this should soon lead to greater efficiency in organisation.

2.4 When they have finished, ask them which of their partner's comments they have agreed with, and which ones they have disagreed with. Urge them to think critically about their partner's advice. Ask them to be specific in giving their reasons for agreement/disagreement. Then they should try to revise/improve their plan.

2.5 They can begin writing when they are ready. The length of time spent on the previous stages will vary widely according to the proficiency and educational backgrounds of the members of the group. Encourage the students to write either in the first person plural (*we*) or in the third person plural (*the group/they*). This is to avoid establishing the habit of writing in the first person singular when writing a report of this type.

Circulate and explain, prompt, elicit or guide as necessary. Students will write at different speeds. If they have not finished at the end of the lesson, they can complete their draft for homework.

 Step 2

It may be best to leave the peer evaluation for the next class, unless you have at least 30–40 minutes of lesson time left.

2.6 Put students into pairs and ask them to discuss each other's drafts. If possible, try to avoid pairing speakers of the same first language. They will tend to organise discourse in similar ways and to make the same errors of language use, and as a result may reinforce each other's errors. If this can not be avoided, emphasise the importance of speaking in English at all times.

The first peer evaluation is likely to take a considerable amount of time, especially for a first exercise with students unfamiliar with the 'process' approach – up to an hour is not unusual with some groups. It will be time well spent, however, and should gradually be reduced with each writing task as students become more familiar with this approach.

2.7 Circulate quietly while they are reading their partner's drafts and answer their questions as necessary. Some students may want further explanation of the evaluation guidelines given in 2.7. Emphasise that they should be looking for *strengths* as well as *weaknesses* in their partner's draft.

2.8 During the discussion, eavesdrop and intervene where necessary. You may need to prompt students. You may need to interpret the evaluation guidelines in 2.7 or the further questions given in 2.8. The main aim is to get the students reading each other's work critically (but not destructively) so that as writers they both give and receive a reader's response.

You may want to remind them of the term *constructive criticism*, which was described in the introductory aims of the Students' Book. If parts of the writing – especially the main ideas – are not clear, they should say so. But they should also consider ways of dealing with the difficulty.

If you note any significant language errors, quietly correct them on the student's drafts without drawing too much attention to them. At this stage they should be concentrating on content, organisation and vocabulary. Many students will need to forget about traditional notions of 'correctness' for the time being in order to achieve fluency in their expression.

2.9 Continue circulating and ask students to answer the critical questions about their partner's comments. Elicit specific reasons for their agreement/disagreement. It is important to encourage this critical sense at an early stage so that the process of peer evaluation leads to independence. It is also useful in making sure that students don't reinforce each other's errors or introduce new ones.

Step 3

2.10 Rewriting the draft will probably have to be done as homework. Emphasise that students should continue the process of revision and improvement on their own draft before they write the final version. There is a risk that some students, especially at an early stage, will rely too heavily on a partner's comments when they revise their work.

2.11 Stress that checking their spelling is a useful exercise, but that they should not worry excessively about it. Some students are likely to attach too much importance to spelling, especially if they have other serious problems in writing in English. A joke or two about the illogicality of English spelling may be reassuring. Students who have access to word processors can make use of 'spell-checking' facilities. It may be worth pointing this out.

Emphasise that you would like to collect and see all the stages in their writing process: brainstorming, plans, first drafts and final drafts. Although only the final draft will be marked, the others stages will provide useful information about how much or how little the students have been able to evaluate, revise and improve their work in this first writing task. This information can be used to make the process of peer evaluation and self-evaluation in Unit 2 more effective.

Discussion

This question is designed to make students more aware of the integrated nature of the Reading and Writing books in this course. Discussion should eventually elicit the fact that the need to maintain independence and critical judgement in approaches to learning, advocated in Reading Unit 1, is one of the assumptions underlying the process approach. You may want to point out that the self-evaluation and peer evaluation processes which they have just completed put learner independence and critical judgement into practice.

If time permits, review what has been covered in this unit. Show the diagram below on the board or overhead projector and explain how it summarises what the students have done in writing their essay. Say that this scheme provides the basis for much of the work that they will be doing on this writing course. It may also be worth pointing out that the scheme is based on research into writing. Some students like the reassurance of knowing that what they are doing has academic respectability.

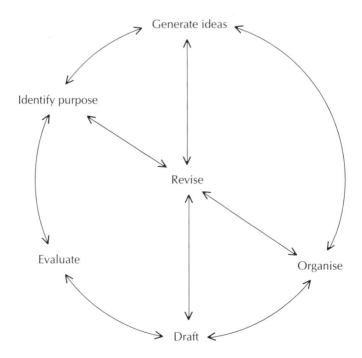

UNIT 2

STUDYING ABROAD

INTRODUCTION

The writing in this unit is relatively demanding for an English for Academic Purposes class at this stage, since it requires students to respond to a stimulus text in the guise of a letter to the editor. It also requires them to distinguish between personal and objective styles of writing, as it is mostly the latter that they will require for their academic studies.

Clearly, this is a long way from describing things, places, and processes. There are, however, reasons for this. The topic – studying abroad – is one that is close to the concerns of all the students, and experience of using this material with other similar groups suggests that it is one that appeals to them. Another reason for doing this piece of writing is that it is a complete text, and the arguments which the students put forward must be logically related to the stimulus text while at the same time having some sort of internal coherence of their own. The completed letter must have a clear opening, a developed main body and a forceful conclusion which should be related to the overall purpose of the writer.

The organisation of ideas in the stimulus text can be used as a framework for the response which the students will write; or they can diverge from this if they wish. On the whole, it is probably best for the students' letters to deal with the points in the order in which they occur in the stimulus text.

Once the students have completed Tasks 1 and 2, they can be divided into groups of between four and six to write group letters containing what they think are the best ideas and expressions from the second drafts in their group. This will promote the aim of developing an awareness of writing within and for a discourse community. Task 4 can be omitted, however, if you feel that the previous work has already taken enough time or if there are problems with the group dynamics.

TASK 1

For this task, it would be a good idea to have in the class an issue of a quality newspaper – not necessarily a current issue – with the *Letters to the editor* page intact. Either bring one in yourself or ask students to do so.

Step 1

1.1 Begin by asking students what they understand by the word *argument*. They may suggest a dispute, disagreement or quarrel. Others may suggest a reason, as in arguments for and against something. Others may put forward the less familiar idea of an abstract or summary. Ask them to write three meanings and to give examples.

Give an example of another meaning of *argument*, such as:

Motor vehicles produce toxic gases. These gases affect the air and people's health. To improve the quality of the air and people's health, we must do something to reduce toxic gases from motor vehicles. One way of doing this would be to reduce the number of cars on the roads.

From an example such as this, move on to the idea of an argument being the use of reason to decide something or persuade someone. Tell students that they are going to write an essay of argument in this last sense about an issue related to themselves.

1.2 Elicit discussion about the differences between *evidence* and *opinion*. Make sure that students understand the examples given. Ask them to identify the words in the right-hand column which express an opinion or value judgement: 'kind and hard-working' and 'too many'.

It may be useful to introduce the words *objective* and *subjective* in this context. Other opposing pairs could be elicited, such as *impartial* and *biased*.

1.3 Ask students to give two further examples of facts contrasted with opinions. It would be a good idea to move around the class discussing these with pairs of students and then to take up examples in plenary on the board or overhead projector. Arrange the further examples in two columns as before, and again ask the group to identify the specific words and phrases on the right which express opinion or value judgement.

Some students may still have trouble distinguishing fact from opinion or vice versa. Continue adding to and analysing the list of examples on the board or overhead projector until you are satisfied that the essential differences are clear to the group.

 Step 2

Ask students why they would want to go abroad to study. Apart from the obvious answers ('I would go/am going to study food science' etc.) probe the reasons why they would go abroad rather than stay in their own countries. This should lead to them to saying that their own countries lack the facilities for postgraduate study in their subject; or that an overseas qualification will give them higher status; or that an overseas qualification opens up international job opportunities; and so on.

1.4 Ask students to read Text 2.1 individually. Briefly explain the convention of letters to the editor and show other examples from the daily newspaper which has been brought to class. Explain that the editor himself or herself may never actually read the letters – a sub-editor in charge of this part of the paper will do this and make a selection. The letters are a way for readers to raise or comment upon issues which will usually have appeared in articles in the newspaper.

Conventionally, the writer addresses the editor as *Dear Sir* and signs *Yours faithfully*. A letter will not be accepted for publication if the writer fails to provide name and address although, at the writer's request, his or her identity can be omitted in the published letter, as is the case here.

1.5 To help students identify the main ideas in Text 2.1, review the first one or two paragraphs in plenary and write the points on the board or overhead projector as follows:

Paragraph	Main idea
1	Unnecessary for students to go abroad to study: good education at home
2	Cultural and intellectal problems: students learn useless information or become confused
3	Language problems: is English useful on return?
4	Cost: better to spend money on facilities at home
5	Studying abroad corrupts the native culture and way of life

1.6, 1.7 Ask students to list the other arguments by themselves, then elicit them and complete the summary on the board or overhead projector.

Explain the use of **finally** and **so** in the last paragraph. **Finally** signals the introduction of the last point in a series of reasons for the writer's argument – in this case, the corruption of the native culture by **immoral** ideas brought back from abroad. **So** signals the writer's overall or global conclusion on the basis of the preceding arguments.

 Step 3

1.8 Most students will be familiar with the concept of cause and effect but some may not be familiar with the terminology. Elicit various possible examples of cause and effect relationships from students. If none are forthcoming, try a simple example on the board or overhead projector, such as:

Because it was raining this morning, I took an umbrella.
I took an umbrella because it was raining this morning.

Point out that the order of cause and effect clauses/sentences can be variable, as in the above examples, where they are reversed. Then ask students to try to contribute examples of their own. Highlighting the cause and effect markers in the examples given can lead into 1.9.

17

1.9 *Because* is the most commonly used marker and will probably have emerged in 1.8. Ask students to produce other cause and effect markers before they consult the lists in Appendix 1 and Sections 5 and 6 of Evaluation Checklist A.

1.10 This exercise should help students to identify many of the underlying assumptions in the letter, and this in turn can lead to more effective counter-arguments in their replies. You may want to give the first example of a cause and effect relationship in the letter to help them.

Paragraph	Sentence	Marker
1	4	and so
2	1	When … then*
	2–3	As a result
	4	because
3	1–2	Therefore
4	2–3	Because of this
5	1–2	For this reason

*A *when … then* construction often implies a degree of cause and effect. In this case *then* is omitted but understood.

1.11 You can introduce the terms *explicit* and *implicit* here to distinguish between the cause and effect relationships which are overtly marked and the one which is not. You may want to make the point that writers can sometimes disguise their assumptions or assertions, consciously or unconsciously, making cause and effect relationships less obvious than they could be, by omitting such indicators. By doing this, writers can avoid accountability for the arguments they are putting forward. (See Appendix 4.)

1.12 Students should be asked to question the validity of each of the relationships they have identified, particularly in relation to the presence or absence of reliable *evidence*. In fact, of course, in Text 2.1 no specific evidence is given for any of the assertions.

Task 2

Students not only need to work on distinguishing evidence from opinion, they also need to work on distinguishing between personal and impersonal styles in writing. Text 2.2 provides an example of the latter, and the work in this task will lead on to more detailed work on personal and impersonal styles and showing or avoiding commitment in Unit 7.

Step 1

Go over the introductory notes and point out that some writers try to persuade by using a personal style which involves the reader, while others try to persuade by using an objective, authoritative style in which they make few or no personal appeals to the reader. Much of the academic writing which students do will probably be of the latter type, although conventions are changing regarding ways in which academic writers identify themselves personally in their writing (see Unit 7).

There are also culturally related differences which affect writing conventions. In some discourse communities, personal argument in academic writing is acceptable, while in others – notably American and British – an objective style is preferred. Students coming from a discourse community in which personal styles of argument are acceptable may find it difficult to adopt a more impersonal style of writing, as exemplified in Text 2.2.

2.1 Ask students to read Text 2.2 individually. When they have read it, encourage them to express their reactions to this version and elicit stylistic comparisons with Text 2.1.

2.2 Text 2.2 contains no more facts than Text 2.1. From this, it is possible to conclude that an objective style may be no more factual than a personal style, even though it may seem more authoritative.

2.3 The differences between Text 2.1 and 2.2 are mainly to do with the degree of personalisation in Text 2.1 through the use of personal pronouns such as *I* and *we* and adjectives such as *our*. Text 2.2. also avoids rhetorical questions, uses noun phrases rather than active verbs and includes less emotive terms.

Text 2.1	Text 2.2
what they teach	their instruction is
our students have to study in a foreign language	another problem faced by this country's students is having to study in a foreign language
our government has less money to spend on education at home	reducing the amount available for education in this country
our students come back with many immoral ideas	students return with ideas which are out of keeping with local values

2.4 Encourage discussion of the two versions of the letter. Students may find Text 2.1 more convincing because it is more personal. Text 2.2 may seem more authoritative because the style is less personal, though it contains no more evidence than Text 2.1 One could conclude that Text 2.1 is more effective for a general readership, while Text 2.2 may be preferred for an academic readership.

TASK 3

Tell the students that they are going to write a response to the original letter, arguing against the writer's views. If you are using the Reading book in this series, remind students that they can refer back to the texts in Unit 2 for ideas if they wish. They should also bear in mind the importance of clear and valid cause and effect relationships as they prepare their counter-arguments.

Emphasise the need for evidence to support their points. You may want to stress that they should try to include evidence of an objective kind from other texts which you or they have located. Where possible, they can also incorporate concrete examples from their own experience of studying abroad. Such experience puts them in an authoritative position although it is not evidence in the strict sense.

 Step 1

3.1 Refer back to the list of topics or main ideas in 1.5.

This is the brainstorming stage. Tell the students to write down quickly their own ideas against the writer's arguments. They should not try to write full or correct sentences – words or phrases will do. And they should use their own language if they can't think of the words in English, and then translate it later. Ideas, not linguistic accuracy, are the priority at this stage.

Discuss these questions in plenary when they have finished their brainstorming:

- Who is going to read my letter?
- What does my reader believe?
- Which ideas are the best points for persuading my reader to agree with my argument?

Establish the point that although the original writer of the letter may read the student's letter, the first person who actually reads it will be the sub-editor. The other readers will be readers of the newspaper, and the purpose of the student writer is to persuade readers away from the views of the original letter-writer. The response which the students are going to write must be closely linked to the original as they are to argue against the views put forward by the original writer.

Note that it is important to think of the reader and what he or she believes. The original writer's beliefs have been made clear in the original letter. We have to assume that a number of other readers are either of a similar viewpoint or uncertain. We want to persuade them to accept our viewpoint.

3.2 Ask students to organise their ideas using the pattern shown in the following table. You may need to start in plenary, using the board or overhead projector, with students nominating the point they wish to make and citing the evidence for it. Emphasise again the importance of giving support to arguments by citing evidence. Many students will be tempted into making an emotive response rather than providing enough concrete support.

Point 1	Evidence
Point 2	Evidence
Point 3	Evidence

You may want to postpone the peer evaluation of plans until Unit 3, especially if your group is less proficient or seems to have initial difficulty in adapting to the 'process' approach. It is also time-consuming to conduct two peer evaluations – on both the plan and the first draft – for the same writing task. Nevertheless, it is suggested that you ask the students to evaluate each other's plans in at least a few of these writing tasks. The time spent on this should soon lead to greater efficiency.

3.3 Circulate and eavesdrop as students discuss and revise their plans. Intervene as necessary to offer guidance, answer questions and so on.

3.4 As in the previous writing task, emphasise the need for careful critical appraisal of what their partner has advised. Continue circulating and engage in individual discussion to ascertain whether or not each student has treated his or her partner's comments critically. Ask them to focus on one major point of disagreement with their partner's advice, and ask them to be specific in rebutting this.

Alternative route

If you find that students don't seem to have enough ideas to formulate a coherent counter-argument to the original letter, try this alternative exercise after 3.1:

1. In groups or in plenary, ask students to take turns at reading out one idea each, going round the group until they have read out all their ideas.

2. Ask the students these questions:
   - Do you find that you have similar ideas?
   - Do some of your ideas go together? For instance, you may all have points on the economic cost of study abroad.
   - Do many of you have ideas on the academic advantages?

3. Tell them to group their ideas together and give each group of ideas a heading.

4. Discuss the evidence they have for some of their ideas. For instance, if they believe that there are economic advantages from studying abroad, what evidence do they have?

 Step 2

Before they begin their first draft, point out that they should begin their own letter by referring to the original letter, using the beginning suggested in the Student's Book, or variants on the following examples:

Dear Sir,
In his/her letter of (date), the anonymous correspondent asks why it is necessary for students to go abroad to study.

Dear Sir,
I wish to respond to the writer/correspondent who criticised the practice of sending students abroad to study.

Remind students that there is a word limit of 500 to 600 words (roughly one and a half to two sides of A4 paper). Letters to the editor are not usually published if they are too long.

3.5 Ask students to write their first draft. The first sentence has been provided in 3.5 of the Student's Book. More proficient groups can do this as homework, especially if the draft has already been started in class. If you feel that your group needs more careful guidance, students can write the first draft during the next class. This will probably take at least one session. Circulate, prompt and help where necessary. Students who have not finished their first draft at the end of the class should do this as homework so that everyone has their first draft ready for the next session.

3.6 Ask the students to do their own preliminary evaluation of their first drafts, with the aid of the post-writing questions listed in the Student's Book.

3.7 Circulate and answer questions as students try to improve their first draft.

 Step 3

Before the students read each other's letters, ask them to suggest what things they will be looking for in what they read. In other words, get them to talk about the criteria they will use in evaluating each other's letters. Refer again to the post-writing questions if necessary.

Introduce Evaluation Checklist A on page 21 of the Student's Book. Elicit questions if they are unsure about any of the terms used (*cohesion* may well need to be explained in detail). Emphasise that they should focus on Sections 2 and 4 at this stage. These sections, on purpose and structure, complement the emphasis on content in the post-writing questions. The evaluation checklist will also seem more manageable if they are only asked to use only a part of it at this stage.

3.8 Ask students to read their drafts aloud to a partner. Elicit reasons why they think this might be a good exercise. Point out that if they speak and hear their own writing, they will be able to identify problems and errors more easily. If the group is very proficient, as an alternative they can exchange and read each other's drafts aloud. This is often even more effective.

3.9 Refer to the post-writing questions in 3.6 in the Student's Book. Emphasise to the students that they must be specific in the points they make in response to their partner's letter. There will still be a tendency at this stage to make overly generalised or subjective comments.

3.10 Remind students to concentrate on Sections 2 and 4 of Evaluation Checklist A. Circulate, eavesdrop and intervene when you judge necessary. Scan and read the students' letters and correct any errors which you decide need attention – but don't 'make a big deal' of them.

3.11 Making written comments on their partner's draft or on another piece of paper will help students to focus more carefully on the criteria being applied. It will also compel them to take more individual responsibility for their comments if they have to commit them to writing. Furthermore, with a written record you will be able to identify problems in the process of peer evaluation more easily.

3.12 Circulate and encourage the process of critical appraisal of each other's comments, as before. Ask them to give specific reasons for agreement/disagreement.

 Step 4

3.13 Refer students once again to Appendix 1 on page 67 and to Evaluation Checklist A on page 21. Go over Sections 5 and 6 if necessary, so that students can apply these criteria on their own before writing their final draft. Encourage students to seek your advice on any points that they aren't sure about – including language points.

3.14 Ask students to write their second draft. This can be completed as homework. Stress that you want them to hand in all of their drafts, including the plan. Try to reassure students who may feel self-conscious or anxious about this that they will only be marked on the basis of their final draft.

TASK 4

This task is optional and can be omitted, particularly if you feel that enough time has been taken with the unit already or if there are problems with the group dynamics in the class.

 Step 1

This is a chain activity. You will probably want to split the class into two or, with less advanced groups, possibly three subgroups to expedite the work.

4.1–4.3 The second drafts are circulated around the group from left to right. In a group of six, for example, each student reads five drafts. Ask the students to read quickly.

Step 2

4.4 Ask the students in each group to nominate a coordinator, who will write down the ideas put forward by the others.

4.5 Each student should offer two ideas for the group letter – one from his or her own draft and one from another person's. The coordinator should assemble these, and each group should discuss how they can be selected and organised. In effect, they have to chose the 'gems' from each other's work. They will have to adapt these as they incorporate them in a group organisation.

4.6 Circulate and advise where necessary. You may want to elicit some of the ideas and write them on the board or overhead projector. If necessary, suggest one or two yourself to facilitate discussion.

4.7 Attempt to identify a general theme or trend in each group's ideas. This general idea can become the thesis – the central idea which is to be expounded – in the group letter. This should not be difficult when students are responding to a stimulus text with a clear thesis to which they have to present a counter-argument. Remind them that it is very important to have a central idea as this gives a focus and coherence to the discourse.

4.8 Refer students again to the main ideas and their sequence in the writer's original letter as a guideline for their organisation.

4.9 Remind students of similar questions and considerations which you presented in 3.1.

 Step 3

4.10 Discuss how students can begin the letter. You may want to elicit ideas and put them on the board or overhead projector. What kind of opening will attract the editor's interest? What will readers want to know first in the letter? The need for a clear statement of thesis can be emphasised.

4.11 There is more than one possible approach here. The suggestion in the Student's Book is that each person in the group can be responsible for one paragraph, and the coordinator can assemble and edit these. You may have other ideas about how you want to approach this.
   Remind students of paragraphing as they proceed. Refer them again to the advice on paragraphing in Task 1, Steps 2 and 3.

4.12 When they are coming to the end, raise the question of how to conclude the report. Ask students to suggest interesting endings. If each student has written one paragraph for the group letter, suggest that they try to compose the conclusion as a group. Remind them of the importance of referring again to their thesis.

UNIT 3

COMPARING AND CONTRASTING CITIES

INTRODUCTION

The work in this unit is basically about comparison and contrast. The topic is related to the texts in Reading Unit 3 on urban development. These texts involve comparison of past and present states – Text 3.1 on the growth of cities opens with a type of comparison: more and more of the world's population are living in towns. This and other comparison types which also occur in Text 3.1 can be referred to if students need examples when they come to their own writing. In fact, the approach to be adopted in this Writing unit (as in others) is not to begin with the linguistic forms of a function such as comparison and then to find a use for them. Rather it is to begin by developing a need for comparison and contrast, and then to find forms of expression.

Some separate grammar notes and references on comparison are provided for your use in an appendix at the end of this unit.

Before you begin the unit you may want to remind students that in English *compare/comparison* can refer to the relationships between things in terms of *either* similarities *or* differences. This is potentially confusing for some students, especially in the collocation *compare and contrast*, where *compare* clearly refers more specifically to similarities. In informal use, however, the word tends to refer more often to differences.

TASK 1

Step 1

The diagrams of 'vertical' and 'horizontal' patterns of comparison/contrast on page 23 of the Student's Book may still prove difficult for some groups, even if they have already seen and applied these in Reading Unit 3. Text 3.1 in this unit on the disposal of radioactive wastes provides a brief example of a 'vertical' pattern.

1.1 Some students may find the content of Text 3.1 difficult at first. You may want to elicit from the group some ideas and vocabulary on this topic before you ask them to read the text. For less proficient groups, skimming followed by discussion and a more careful second reading may be more appropriate.

1.2 Possible answers to the questions are as follows:

(a) The description is based on a contrast of different methods of disposing of radioactive waste.

(b) 'Vertical', although the order of points does not closely correspond.

(c) **however** in sentence 6, **instead** in sentence 7 and **Furthermore** in sentence 5.

Try to elicit synonyms for these three words before students consult the list in Appendix 1.

 Step 2

This exercise should help to consolidate students' understanding of the 'vertical' and 'horizontal' patterns of organisation. Ask the students to work in pairs. Circulate and offer guidance as needed. You may want to elicit some initial ideas about how to begin and put them on the board or overhead projector, especially if there are problems. You may also want to emphasise, especially with weaker groups, that it is not necessary to rearrange the order of *all* eight sentences. Be alert for students who may also try to rewrite or summarise the sentences, which is unnecessary and time-consuming.

1.3 Suggest either of the following new orders:

- 1   2   3   4   6   5   7   8
- 1   2   3   4   6 and 7a   5   7b   8

Sentences 5, 6 and 7 can be reworded in various ways to accommodate the new 'horizontal' pattern. One possible approach is as follows:

(6) In other European countries, however, large salt domes do not exist, and the problem was ignored for about two decades.

(5) The concept of a 'dry' repository became the basis of research into disposal until the late 1970s in countries with these deposits.

(7) On the other hand, European countries without these chose instead, from the mid-seventies, to look at crystalline rock-types.

1.4 Circulate and offer guidance as needed. Some groups have considerable difficulty with this exercise, but once they have completed it they should be able to produce either pattern effectively in their own writing.

It may be useful to ask students either to hand in this exercise for you to read at this point or to hand it in with their drafts at the end of Task 3. The first option will help to reveal any serious problems with this function *before* students begin the writing task in Task 3.

It would also be helpful to consider some of the 'input' on comparison and contrast in Appendix 2 so that students are not misled by the apparent simplicity and straightforwardness of the language given.

Pair work in the production of further examples may be appropriate.

Task 2

 Step 1

In Step 1 the students are asked to consider the characteristics of two towns or cities in order to compare and contrast them. It will depend on the students' study situation whether or not they compare the towns they are studying in now with their home towns. Pair students so that comparisons they make in peer evaluation will be unproblematic. Begin with a discussion of the differences between the two cities they have chosen.

2.1 Ask students to write down answers to the two questions in their books. It is important that they all write something. This is to prevent some students acting as 'passengers' in the subsequent discussion.

2.2 When they have written notes in response to the questions, encourage discussion in small groups, or, if you prefer, turn it into a plenary exchange of points.

The idea now is to move from the specific points which students will have listed to the development of general categories. These categories will provide a basis for organising ideas in the writing which the students will do, while the specific points that they have written down will provide examples and detailed content.

 Step 2

2.3 Provide further examples of general categories and specific instances if the students are unsure of what to do. With students contributing, group the specific examples in the Student's Book under three headings on the board:

- Location
- Population
- Industries

2.4 Proceed with a discussion of other headings or categories which students themselves may have produced or which are needed. You can stimulate more thought and discussion by asking them to think of the things that they would want to know about a town, or about the towns of other members of the class. Phrasing the points as questions can help to produce further ideas.

Encourage students to organise their information by using diagrams similar to those shown in the Student's Book.

2.5 Circulate and assist with or contribute to the students' discussion if they are slow to produce further ideas. There can be a tendency in some groups for students to limit themselves to the categories already suggested in their books.

2.6 Continue to circulate and intervene or answer questions as students make the lists of all their main headings. Encourage them to expand the specific points and examples which will support or develop the main ideas.

 Step 3

2.7 To get the idea across, you can start by building up a table on the board or overhead projector, with students contributing. If they have already got the idea, however, let them continue to work on their own individual tables.

Emphasise that the categories given in the table in the Student's Book are only examples and do not have to be followed. If necessary, continue to elicit other categories, such as 'History', 'Problems resulting from development', etc. Warn the students to leave plenty of space for each category and the information that is to go in the other two columns.

2.8 Encourage students to complete their tables with specific points to support or develop their information.

2.9 When the tables are completed, go on to discuss why they might write a comparison of their two towns. Possibly they will already have done something like this in letters home.

Encourage them to think about who they would write for. It is important to consider both purpose and audience, as these will influence the content and organisation of what they write. It can be assumed, for instance, that readers of a different nationality will know relatively little about the writer's own town, so certain information will have to be given which could be safely omitted for an audience already familiar with the subject.

2.10 The discussion can be conducted in pairs and/or in plenary. Students are likely to lack some of the information they need. This means they will need to carry out a minor form of library research. Refer students to extra sources of information if they need it. They will not need highly detailed and extensive information as their essays won't be very long. But they may need to find out something about industries, history or civic amenities. They should bring any new information to the next session, having read it through themselves beforehand.

TASK 3

In this task, students should write and evaluate their first draft. They should aim to write approximately 500 words. If there are students who can easily write more than this, don't discourage them. An upper limit of around 700 words, however, would encourage them to be concise and organised in their approach.

Step 1

Refer back to Task 2 and briefly review what was done. Remind students about the extra information they were asked to bring to this session.

3.1 Discuss who they are going to write for and why they are writing, using the questions in 3.1 of the Student's Book.

In Unit 2 they were given a specific form and context for publication as a 'letter to the editor' in an (imagined) overseas newspaper. For this writing exercise they will have to decide for themselves on the form of publication and distribution and the country – Britain or their own country.

Try to elicit ideas for the context from the students. Possible examples in either Britain or their own country could include:

- a local newspaper
- a university publication
- a national newspaper
- a newsletter or journal of a society devoted to international cooperation/trade/ exchange
- an embassy publication designed to brief students planning to study in Britain.

Less confident or less proficient groups can be given the simpler option of writing a letter to you. Even then, it's worth reminding them that you would like to receive an interesting piece of writing.

The purpose of writing can take many forms. Remind students of the instances in both the Reading and Writing books in which they have had to consider a writer's purpose in terms of informing or persuading (or both). For example, do they want to persuade their readers to visit either city? Do they want to persuade their readers of the serious nature of problems with urban development? Or do they simply wish to inform interested readers?

What will be the central idea – or thesis – to emerge in their comparison or contrast? It could be a personal one, such as 'home is best'. Or it could be an academic one, such as the influence of transport routes on urban development.

3.2 Circulate and encourage students to ask questions or articulate their decisions in response to the questions in 3.1.

3.3 As students think about and discuss the pre-writing questions (3.3 in the Student's Book), try to move the discussion towards the more academic end of the audience/ purpose continuum. If there are social science students in the class, invite them to consider the kind of audience and purpose relevant to a comparison of the two towns concerned.

Discuss the specific aspects to be compared – for example:

- the history of urban development in the two places concerned
- features of industrial development
- the development of public services
- problems arising from urban expansion.

Step 2

3.4 Point out to students that in the tables they completed in 2.7 they have the basis for their essays. They should now begin to develop their tables into workable essay plans.

After they have had some time to think, you can circulate and encourage them to articulate their answers to the five questions in 3.4 in the Student's Book. They will need to decide:

- which items will be most relevant to their purpose and audience
- the most effective order for both their categories and individual points
- which pattern – vertical or horizontal – they prefer to use
- the subject of their thesis.

3.5 Circulate, eavesdrop and intervene as necessary in the exchange and evaluation of plans. Remind students of the need for *balanced* criticism in terms of both strengths and weaknesses.

The need to make these comments in writing will encourage students to be more focused and careful in their approach.

3.6 Encourage students to think critically about their partner's comments and to give specific reasons for agreement/disagreement. Ask them how they intend to improve/ have improved their plans. Make sure that they have a clear understanding of either a vertical or a horizontal pattern of organisation in relation to their essay and intend to use one or the other consistently.

Step 3

Before they begin writing, explain to the students that you will be on hand to help them during their drafting. If they are uncertain about something, they can ask you.

Encourage them to write quickly so as not to get 'bogged down' with the mechanics of writing, such as spelling. Remind them that as they are writing a first draft, there are plenty of opportunities for improvement and refinement once the first draft is completed.

3.7 Before they begin writing ask the students to consider the markers of comparison and contrast in Appendix 2 at the back of the Student's Book.

3.8 Ask students to begin writing their first draft. Let them get on with writing and, once they are well embarked on the process, circulate around the class, reading what they have written and prompting as necessary. If students seem to need help, ask questions like:

- What is the connection between A and B?
- What will you write about next?
- What is the main idea in this paragraph?
- Can you explain this point?

If there are major linguistic errors which make the text incomprehensible, ask the student to explain or paraphrase what they have written and then correct the mistake.

3.9 Refer students to the post-writing questions in 3.9 in the Student's Book and ask them to carry out a preliminary evaluation of their own drafts before they exchange drafts with a partner. Circulate and help them apply the questions as appropriate. If it seems necessary, discuss the post-writing questions in plenary so that students feel more confident about their understanding of them.

You may also want some plenary discussion of the results of this initial evaluation before you go on to the next step. Encourage students to describe some of the problems they have had with their draft to the rest of the class.

 Step 4

Introduce Evaluation Checklist B which appears on page 29 of the Student's Book. Take the students through Sections 2 and 3 on organisation and cohesion, to make sure that they understand the points listed. Then work through Sections 4 and 6 on vocabulary and mechanical accuracy, which they will apply in Step 5. Ask them to read Section 5 on grammar for homework and deal with questions in the next class.

Evaluation Checklist B is sometimes felt to be more suitable for more confident or more proficient students. However, it would be a good idea to familiarise them with Evaluation Checklist A as well, so that they have the option of using either checklist in future writing exercises.

3.10 Arrange students in pairs and ask them to exchange drafts with their partner. (You may want to ask them to read their own draft aloud to their partner first.) They should read the draft right through and then, referring to the actual text, they should discuss each other's drafts.

3.11 Refer students to the post-writing questions in 3.9 in the Student's Book and encourage a specific focus on these as you circulate. Most of them deal with content.

3.12 Refer students to Sections 2 and 3 of Evaluation Checklist B. These sections, on organisation and cohesion, complement the post-writing questions. Ask students to apply them to their partner's drafts. Circulate and encourage specific responses to these questions where appropriate. Make it clear, however, that students do not have to write something about *all* of the points in these sections. They should aim to be selective and begin to learn when to invoke and when not to invoke them.

3.13 Once again, encourage students to be detailed and specific in what they write. Ask them also to be sensitive to their partner's preference as to whether the comments are made on the first draft or an another piece of paper. Some students may feel that their draft has been 'spoiled' if someone else writes on it.

3.14 Circulate and monitor the discussion. Remind students of the need for critical evaluation of their partner's comments, as in 3.6. Encourage them to think carefully about whether or not they agree with each of their partner's suggestions, and why. Circulate and ask them to articulate their reasons for agreement/ disagreement clearly. This should help to prevent students reinforcing or contributing to other students' errors, especially in less proficient groups. Point out items which may have been overlooked in their evaluation of each other's drafts.

Alternative route

For less proficient groups, use this alternative route before you go on to Step 5.

1. Collect the evaluated first drafts and read them.

2. Focus on the affirmative – what you have learnt about their own towns and cities, the interesting points of contrast which they chose to deal with, and so on.

3. Review the points which you noted in your reading. Don't deal with more than a few points, and focus only on those which most significantly affect the clarity and coherence of the text. These are likely to include:

   • Beginning and concluding effectively.

   • Re-ordering, cutting or adding information.

   • Comparing and contrasting things which logically can be contrasted or compared.

   • Making comparisons and contrasts clearer through the appropriate use of contrastive devices, such as the ones listed in Appendix 2.

   • Reducing repetition and redundancy, either of information or expression.

   • Paragraphing: splitting 'mega' paragraphs into shorter ones; combining 'mini' paragraphs into longer ones.

   • Splitting or combining sentences. Strings of short sentences can be combined, using relative clauses and other forms of combining.

   Do some examples on the board. Elicit student suggestions.

4. Return first drafts to students and invite them to ask advice on language errors that you have highlighted.

5. Ask students to write their second drafts, incorporating the improvements that have been discussed. Circulate and advise.

6. *Optional.* At the end of the session, students could exchange their second drafts and for homework read their partner's text and write a brief response to it. In their response, they should include:

    • what they found interesting
    • how the points that their partner focused on compare with their own.

 Step 5

3.15 Circulate and assist with this final revision before the second draft is written. Another evaluation with reference to Sections 4 and 6 of Evaluation Checklist B should lead to further improvement and help students avoid relying too heavily on their partner's comments.

3.16 Ask the students to write their second draft. This may have to be done as homework. Conclude the class with a brief plenary discussion of their work, asking the following questions:

• What has proved to be the most difficult part of writing this essay?
• What aspect of the essay or of the writing process are they most happy with?

Evaluation Checklists A and B should be retained by students and referred to whenever they write. Students can be told that these checklists can be applied to anything they write, whether it is part of an intensive English programme or part of their degree course. As writers, they need to look at their own writing from the reader's viewpoint, and the checklists are a way of helping to develop this critical awareness.

Follow-up

Collect students' plans, first drafts and final drafts. Read them and assess how the essay has developed through its stages. Note aspects of good organisation, effective opening and concluding paragraphs, and expression. Also note areas where improvements could be made in organisation or expression, notably to make comparisons and contrasts clearer or to highlight the thesis. You may want to use a highlighter to underline linguistic errors. If there are errors in comparative structures, refer students to the relevant pages of a good students' grammar.

If you feel that more structured guidance is needed on some of the organisational aspects of writing comparisons and contrasts, refer students again to the exercises in Reading Unit 3 and in Task 2 of this unit. Remind them of the 'vertical' and 'horizontal' patterns of comparison/contrast depicted at the beginning of Unit 3 and to the 'input' on the language of comparison and contrast in Appendix 2 in the Student's Book.

If you find that there is very little development or improvement between the first and second drafts, an individual conference with the student concerned may be helpful. Even at this stage some students may resist the need to rewrite, especially if this has never been a part of their academic culture.

APPENDIX: COMPARISON

See Woods, E. and McLeod, N. (1990) *Using English Grammar*, Prentice Hall International, Hemel Hempstead (Unit 4.2–4.5) or Murphy, R. (1985) *English Grammar in Use*, CUP, Cambridge (Units 101–104).

The notes below are based on Leech, G. and Svartvik, J. (1975) *A Communicative Grammar of English*, Longman, London.

Equal comparisons

X *is as* adj *as* Y (*is*)
X *is not as* adj *as* Y (*is*)
X *is not so* adj *as* Y (*is*)

Comparative and superlative

X *is the* adj + *-er of the two.* (two things compared)

X *is the* adj + *-est of the three.* (three or more things compared)

X *is the* adj + *-est of the* Ys.
  e.g. Luxembourg is the smallest of the Common Market countries.

Of the Xs, Y *is   the* adj + *-est* (+ noun).
           has   the most adj (+ noun).
        (etc.)   the most + noun
  e.g. Of all the capital cities in the world, this is the most exotic.
        Of all the capital cities in the world, this has the fastest subway system.
X *is the* adj + *-est in the* Y.
  e.g. Sao Paolo is the fastest growing city in Latin America.

The X's adj + *-est* Y.
  e.g. The world's largest city

Comparison using *than*

Add an element beginning with *than* after the comparative word.
  e.g. The proportion of people living in cities was always **smaller** *than the proportion of the workforce working in factories.*

The item in **bold** is the comparison word. The element beginning with *than* specifies the second part of the comparison.

Comparative phrases

Elements of a subclause can be omitted if they repeat the information in the main clause. If these elements are omitted, we are left with a comparative phrase rather than a comparative clause. That is, *than* is more like a preposition than a conjunction.

> *e.g. There are more pubs than shops in this village.*

Adverbials such as *ever, usual* can follow *than* in comparative phrases.

> *e.g. There were more people on the beach than usual.*

Comparison using *whereas, while, although*

> *e.g. Whereas Reading is built in a valley, Toledo is built on a hill.*
> *While Toronto has a coherent public transport policy, London has none.*
> *Although Milan has an excellent public transport system, it lacks the many open spaces typical of London.*

Comparison with an unstated earlier state or condition

> *e.g. Nowadays food is more expensive (than it used to be).*
> *Foreign cars are becoming more popular (than they were).*

Postponement of the comparative clause from the word it postmodifies

> *e.g. More people own houses these days than used to years ago.*

To indicate continuing change

X *is getting* adj + *-er* and adj + *-er.*
> *e.g. Traffic in London is getting slower and slower.*

Quantifiers as subject: quantifier and quantifier

> *e.g. More and more of the world's population is living in towns and cities.*
> *Fewer and fewer people are using public transport.*

Enough and *too*

To indicate sufficiency and excess.
> *e.g. It was hot enough to melt the tar on the roads.*
> *It was too hot to go out.*
> *It was too hot for comfort.*

So ... (that) and such ... (that)

Similar meaning to *enough* and *too*.

   e.g. *Urban growth in some cities is so great that existing services cannot cope with the increase in numbers.*

Proportion

   e.g. *As time went on, things got worse and worse.*
   As you go further north, so the winters become longer and more severe.

The + a comparative word

   e.g. *The farther north you go, the more severe the winters are.*
   The faster the rate of immigration, the worse the problems become.

UNIT 4

GLOBAL WARMING

INTRODUCTION

In Reading Unit 4 students read about the problem of global warming. As a result, they should now have quite a few ideas on this topic. They should also realise that there are many uncertainties associated with climate changes and that the changes take a long time.

In this unit, students will be using the **Situation→Problem→Solution→ Evaluation** pattern which they have already been introduced to in Reading Unit 4.

TASK 1

 Step 1

Ask students to write down two things that they can remember about global warming from Reading Unit 4. In plenary, ask each student to contribute an idea. Note the ideas on the board or overhead projector and continue eliciting until everyone has contributed at least one idea. Make sure that students do not repeat an idea but contribute one that has not already been suggested.

1.1 Ask students to answer the questions which appear in the Student's Book:

- What are the causes of global warming?
- What problems will global warming lead to?
- What are possible solutions to these problems?

Answers should include the following:

- **Causes**: increased greenhouse gas emissions, notably carbon dioxide and CFC emissions.
- **Problems**: climatic change and rise in sea levels as Arctic ice melts, leading to flooding in low-lying countries, desertification in others, and massive food shortages, famine and a struggle for resources.

 • **Solutions**: reduce greenhouse gas emissions, especially carbon dioxide and CFCs.

1.2 Refer students to the Figures 1–3 in the Student's Book:

 Figure 1: Contribution of greenhouse gases to climate change
 Figure 2: Greenhouse gases and sea levels
 Figure 3: Sources of gases

 Ask students to interpret the information in the figures. Discuss the figures in turn and elicit the students' understanding of them before they go on to answer the questions. If there seem to be problems, the first one or two questions can be discussed in plenary before students try the others on their own.
 The following answers are suggested:

 1. Carbon dioxide
 2. Carbon dioxide
 3. CFCs and HCFCs
 4. CFCs and HCFCs
 5. Coolants for refrigerators and air conditioners; foam-blowing agents; electronics; solvents; aerosols
 6. Burning fossil fuels and forests; cement-making
 7. Approximately 30–35 cm
 8. Methane (cuts of only 15–20 per cent are needed to stabilise concentrations)

1.3 Point out that one of the major sources of toxic gases is the motor vehicle. Burning fossil fuel, i.e. petrol, produces nitrous oxide. As Figure 1 shows, this has a global warming potential of 290. It is also a major contributor to acid rain, which has a harmful effect on plant and animal life.

 Step 2

1.4 Remind students of the work done in Reading Unit 4. Check their understanding of the brief example of the **Situation→Problem→Solution→Evaluation** pattern in 1.4. Ask students to produce another brief example, either of their own choosing or on a topic suggested by you.

1.5 Text 4.1 provides further information about global warming and a more complicated example of the **Situation→Problem→Solution→Evaluation** pattern.
 Ask students to read Text 4.1 and to think about these questions:

 • What is the problem?
 • What is the solution?
 • What are the results of the solution?

 This article – and the other articles that students have already read on the subject – will reveal that for every solution there is another problem.

1.6 Ask the students to work in pairs to complete the flow diagram. This is a possible response:

Situation	Stratospheric ozone layer depletion is even more serious than was previously thought.

⬇

Problem	Greater risks of skin cancer, crop damage, health effects, breaking of vital links in food chains.

⬇

Solution(s)	Developed and developing countries will have to work together to reach a solution.

⬇

Evaluation	Additional financial incentives and a more flexible approach to carrying out the Montreal Protocol will help developing countries accelerate the phasing out of chemicals known to damage the ozone layer.

1.7 Circulate and monitor the discussion. Deal with questions and problems as they arise.

1.8 Ask the students what further problems might be created by the proposed solution in Text 4.1. For example:

> **Problem 2**: Phasing out the use of certain chemicals will close some industries in developing countries and/or make it necessary for them to adapt to new manufacturing. This will lead to unemployment.

> **Solution 2**: Create new industries to replace those which will be phased out, help others to adapt.

> **Evaluation 2**: There will be economic and social problems before this can be done. Financial aid will probably have to be obtained from the developed world.

 Step 3

1.9 Ask the students to rearrange the eight sentences in Text 4.2 so that they follow the **Situation→Problem→Solution→Evaluation** pattern. You may need to elicit some of the vocabulary items before they begin.

Ask them to work individually and then to compare their answers with those of a partner. Less proficient groups can work in pairs from the outset.

Draw their attention to the reference items found at the opening of sentences 1, 3, 4, 5, 6 and 7 (e.g. **To combat this**). These provide significant clues to the original order of the sentences.

The original order of the sentences was:

Paragraph 1 (2), (5), (7)   *Situation and Problem*
Paragraph 2 (1), (3)   *Solution (and Evaluation)*
Paragraph 3 (4), (6), (8)   *Evaluation*

1.10–1.11   Circulate and monitor the discussion. Deal with problems and questions as necessary.

In terms of paragraph groupings, it would be equally possible for students to arrange the sentences as follows:

Paragraph 1 (2)   *Situation*
Paragraph 2 (5), (7)   *Problem*
Paragraph 3 (1)   *Solution*
Paragraph 4 (3), (4), (6), (8)   *Evaluation*

End the activity by telling students that in the next activity they will write the first draft of an article on the following topic:

> **Reducing global warming: what each individual can do**

Remind them to look back over the texts on global warming in Reading Unit 4 and to bring this material with them to the next writing session.

TASK 2

Review Task 1. Ask students to give examples of the **Situation→Problem→Solution→Evaluation** sequences which you dealt with.

To lead into the writing task, you can point out that solutions to the problems of global warming can only start with individuals. What is needed are some immediate, practical solutions which all of us can apply in our daily lives. Elicit some possible ideas about how this could be done.

Explain again that students are to write the first draft of an article on the following topic:

> **Reducing global warming: what each individual can do**

The article is to appear in a student magazine and is to be read by people like the students. It should:

- inform readers of the problem
- suggest some possible solutions
- suggest how these solutions also give rise to other problems
- suggest how each individual can help in his or her daily life.

About 500 words is an appropriate length. Tell students to use the ideas that were discussed in Task 1 together with information and ideas from Reading Unit 4 (which they should have brought to the session). Emphasise that they should use these sources to provide *evidence* for the statements that they make. Remind them to follow the **Situation→Problem→Solution→Evaluation** sequence in their article.

Questions about readership should arise here – in what context or in what country will the student magazine be published? This will make a considerable difference to the knowledge, attitudes and expectations of readers. Decisions about this can be made at either group or individual level. Remind students of similar decisions which they made in Unit 3. Ask them to commit themselves to a decision before they begin to brainstorm and plan their articles.

 ## Step 1

2.1 Draw students' attention to the six pre-writing questions in 2.1 of the Student's Book. Ask them to think about these and to make notes as they do so.

2.2 These questions can be discussed in pairs and/or in a plenary session.

 ## Step 2

2.3 Ask students to brainstorm. Again remind them of the importance of using rough notes rather than complete sentences. Set a time limit if you think this will help to achieve spontaneity and speed. If they have reviewed the texts in the Reading book, they should be ready with ideas.

2.4 Ask students to begin planning their essay by developing and rearranging the results of their brainstorming session. The guidelines should help them to formulate a more effective plan.

2.5 Circulate and prompt where you feel it is needed.

2.6 Continue circulating and engage in individual discussion to ascertain whether or not each student has treated his or her partner's comments critically. Make sure that misguided advice does not lead to extraneous problems in otherwise adequate plans.

 ## Step 3

Suggest that students begin their articles in an interesting and provocative way and that they end in a way which brings the reader back to the beginning.

2.7 Ask them to begin writing their first draft. As they write, circulate and intervene where necessary. Question and prompt the students if they seem stuck but avoid interfering.

2.8 After they have finished writing, ask students to carry out preliminary evaluation of their own drafts with the aid of the post-writing questions in 2.8 of the Student's Book. Encourage them not to consult with each other at this stage so that they don't become too dependent on a partner's advice. Circulate and assist as necessary. If students seem to need or want assistance at this stage, read through parts of completed drafts and encourage them to discuss some of their preliminary evaluation with you. You may want some plenary discussion of the results of this initial evaluation before you go on to the next step. Encourage students to describe to the rest of the class some of the problems they have met when writing their first draft.

 Step 4

2.9 Ask students to exchange drafts and to read their partner's draft carefully.

2.10 After students have read their partner's draft, ask them to apply the post-writing questions in 2.10. Whether the students use Evaluation Checklist A or B will depend on a number of factors, such as the level and needs of the group, your own preference and the students' preferences. Evaluation Checklist A may be more suitable at first for less proficient groups.

You may want to encourage students to try Evaluation Checklist B again with this writing exercise so that they become more familiar with it. Some students may still be daunted by its length and apparent complexity. Again, selective use of one of the evaluation checklists is advisable here. Both checklists will be consulted again in Step 5, with a different emphasis for each one.

2.11 Ask students to apply the points in the specified sections of Evaluation Checklist A or B.

2.12 Again stress the importance of making detailed written comments, either on their partner's draft or on another piece of paper. If some students would prefer to do this after the discussion, this is acceptable as long as the written comments are made in detail.

2.13 Circulate and monitor the process of discussion. Answer questions and deal with problems, as necessary. To provide additional help, especially to weaker groups, you may want to summarise in plenary the main points that have emerged from their discussions with each other. If there are problems which most students are experiencing, deal with them on the board or overhead projector.

As in 2.6, ask students individually how they have evaluated their partner's comments and for what reasons. If the class is large and time is limited, a possible approach is to ask each student to describe in detail *one* comment with which he or she disagrees and to say why. Resolution of one point may enable this student to deal with other points more confidently.

 Step 5

2.14 After the peer evaluation has been completed, encourage students to continue to work on their drafts before they rewrite. Circulate and offer guidance with the use of either of the evaluation checklists if needed. The sections specified in the Student's Book (Sections 5 and 6 of Evaluation Checklist A and Sections 4 and 6 of Evaluation Checklist B) provide further guidelines.

2.15 The final draft will probably be produced as homework, as in previous units, unless you feel that further monitoring is necessary. Collect all the drafts and, as before, emphasise that students should hand in all the written stages of their writing process: brainstorming, plans, first drafts and final drafts. You may want to stress again to students that only the final draft will be marked.

If you find too little evidence of evaluation and development from one stage to another in an essay, an individual conference with the student concerned may be advisable. By the end of this unit students should be reasonably confident and efficient in both self-evaluation and peer evaluation.

Task 3 (optional)

Writing conference

This is the first opportunity for students to take a global look at their writing and to try to identify consistent patterns of both error and effectiveness in what they write. Until now they will have considered only individual essays.

Whether you do this activity or not will depend on several factors:

- the size of your class
- the time available
- the language proficiency of the group
- the extent to which students have generally adapted to the 'process' approach
- their confidence and fluency in using the metalanguage of critical evaluation.

If you feel that any of these factors raises serious problems, it may be best either to omit this activity altogether or to postpone it until the completion of Unit 5 or Unit 6. Another option is to deal with the more confident or proficient students in the group when you have reached the end of Unit 4 and to arrange appointments with other students at the end of Unit 5. You may also want to make this activity optional within the group. Those students who are not interested need not feel compelled to take part.

Emphasise that students should look for strengths and weaknesses that occur in *at least two essays*. Remind them that isolated points occurring in one essay only can be overlooked.

The conference is essentially concerned with a comparison of the students' self-assessment, in terms of strengths and weaknesses, with the essays they have evaluated. Some students by this time will be reasonably accurate in their assessment. You may find that some students are able to put little or nothing under the 'Strengths' column. This will provide an opportunity both to encourage a more balanced view of their work and to boost their morale.

The recommended length of time for this conference is about 15 minutes, although some students may need slightly longer than this.

It would be a good idea to emphasise that students should hand in both the detailed self-assessment on a sheet of A4 and the essays they have chosen for evaluation *the day before* they come to the writing conference. This will give you an opportunity to compare their written self-assessment with their essays and to identify discrepancies. It will also avoid wasting time if students are not adequately prepared. In this exercise some students may want to assume more of a 'passenger' role and wait for words of wisdom instead of carrying out an analysis of their own. If their self-assessmemt seems skimpy or hastily done when they hand it in, ask them to try again and arrange another appointment to discuss it.

This exercise will also help to reveal the extent to which students follow up and make use of your written feedback on their essays. If you find that this is not happening, suggest strategies for this so that they can learn more effectively from their mistakes when essays are returned to them.

UNIT 5

YOUR ACADEMIC SUBJECT

TASK 1

Introduce this unit by referring back to Reading Units 4 and 5, in which students worked on definitions, and to Writing Unit 3, in which some work may have been done on classification. Both of these language functions will be of use in the work in this unit which is on the topic:

> **Define and justify your subject or profession**

Tell students that this is the topic and that they are to carry out some preparatory activities before drafting their own individual essays.

 Step 1

1.1 Ask students to consider the definition below. Ask them if there is any extra information that they might need in order to make sense of the definition.

> *Psycholinguistics: A branch of linguistics which studies the correlation between linguistic behaviour and the psychological processes thought to underlie that behaviour.*
>
> From Crystal, D. (ed.) 1980, *A First Dictionary of Linguistics and Phonetics*, Longman, London

1.2 Ask students to make notes on this and discuss their ideas with a partner. The question of readership is important here and ideas about this should be elicited before they have gone very far. They should also consider the needs of a non-specialist reader.

Discuss with the group as a whole the appropriateness of the definition for a non-specialist reader and what information should be added or clarified.

1.3 Organise students into small groups of three or four, mixed according to subjects or professions. If possible, no two people in a group should be studying the same subject or belong to the same profession.

Tell students that they are to write a formal definition of their subject or profession for the other members of the group. Refer back to work in Reading Units 4 and 5 for models. You may also want to remind them of the work done on categorising in Unit 3 of this book and the classification diagram which was given as an example. Other forms of this can be illustrated on the board or overhead projector. Students may want to organise their ideas in this way before they write their definitions.

Students can compare their core definitions. It may be a good idea at this point to ask for two or three suggestions and put them on the board or overhead projector for group comment.

1.4 Ask students to expand their core definitions into a short paragraph of extended definition which would make it clear to a non-specialist. ·

1.5 Ask students to exchange extended definitions with at least one other person in their group and to ask each other the questions listed in 1.5 in the Student's Book.

Elicit some extended definitions and write them on the board or overhead projector. Discuss and improve them.

 Step 2

1.6, 1.7 Ask students to write a concise account of what the term *justifying* means, as it would be used in an academic context. Ask them to compare their definition with another person's formulation.

Elicit their definitions. One formulation is as follows:

To give a good reason for; to explain satisfactorily.

There are three possible routes which you could take at this point, depending on the language level and sophistication of your class and your own preferences.

Route A
1. Discuss with students how English language teaching as a professional field can be justified. List points on the board or overhead projector.

2. Discuss some of the assumptions that may lie behind the justification. For instance, the teaching of English may be justified on the grounds that the majority of the world's scientific and technological literature is published in English. One of the assumptions behind this is that having a common language for such literature facilitates communication among a linguistically diverse community of scholars and experts.

3. However, you may wish to go on to consider that the linguistic hegemony enjoyed by English is matched by a hegemony on knowledge. Only those who have English can have easy access to this information, both as receivers and contributors. This then leads to such questions as the following:

   • What does this suggest about the relationship between the English language and control of knowledge and power?
   • Is the use of English a means of maintaining and reproducing a relationship of dependency between the developed world and the underdeveloped world?

- What counter-arguments can be made towards the accusations implied in these questions?

Route B

1. Ask students to suggest on what basis they would justify their own subject or profession to someone who believed that it was unnecessary or even harmful. What arguments and evidence would they put forward in support or justification of their subject? They can discuss this in their groups.

2. Elicit ideas from the groups and combine them on the board or overhead projector. What kinds of argument are being made?

Route C

1. Ask students to make a list of points (economic, political or ethical) which they could use to criticise a subject or profession. Take a subject such as automobile engineering which is related to one of the main sources of atmospheric pollution and global warming. They could also consider:

   - controversial research in one of the sciences
   - the scientific validity of one of the social sciences
   - the value in 'real life' of studying an arts subject.

   To stimulate discussion, you could ask whether subjects or professions are as politically neutral as is claimed. You could also raise questions about vested interests (see the question sheet on page 44 of the Student's Book).

2. Make a list of these points and ask students to consider how they would rebut them in relation to their own subject or profession.

 ## Step 3

1.8 Refer students to the question sheet on page 44 of the Student's Book.

1.9 Elicit and explain the meaning of any vocabulary on the question sheet which you feel may be unfamiliar to your group. Then choose from the following options:

Route A

Go through the questions in relation to English language teaching, with or without recourse to the essay 'Justifying English language teaching' in Task 2 below.

Route B

Ask students to suggest answers in relation to their own subject or profession.

Route C

Ask students to suggest answers in relation to automobile engineering or another subject. Compare the work already done on global warming and the contribution of the motor vehicle to this.

End by asking students to give some further thought to the points on the question sheet in relation to their subject so that they will have some ideas for their first draft in Task 2. Possible answers are given on page 53 of this book.

Task 2

Sample essay

Justifying English language teaching

English language teaching, or ELT, is the profession concerned with the teaching of English to speakers of other languages. Drawing heavily on theory and research in applied linguistics, ELT has developed a body of knowledge about the structure of English and the ways in which languages are learnt. ELT has also developed a set of principles for designing courses and preparing teaching materials. In addition, ELT has evolved a range of teaching methods and assessment procedures. Some methods, such as community language learning, suggestopaedia and 'The Silent Way' have not achieved widespread acceptance, however, because they do not fit in with mainstream ideas in ELT.

Although unorthodox methodologies remain on the fringe, ELT is open to ideas from many disciplines, and from time to time assumptions are challenged by applied linguists, educationists and other academics. Sometimes, too, politicians, administrators and members of the public will question the assumptions and methods of ELT practitioners. This does not always have much effect, however, because the ELT community usually unites in the face of such challenges.

It must also be acknowledged that there are a number of vested interests in ELT, of which publishing, the private language schools and British foreign policy are the most significant. These vested interests prefer stability rather than radical change and so resist challenges to existing knowledge and practices. This means that developments in ELT are evolutionary rather than revolutionary.

As far as ordinary British citizens are concerned, ELT is associated with the thousands of foreign students who come to this country to learn English. In fact, ELT provides the basis of a very large industry worth about £1 billion a year to the British economy, and people from the UK are directly or indirectly service providers in this industry. Students of English, by contrast, are consumers of ELT and they benefit from the improvements in methods and materials developed by ELT specialists.

It could be argued that ELT contributes to the monopoly which English-speaking cultures have on scientific and technical knowledge. However, by providing access to that knowledge, ELT contributes to international relations and national development and so justifies itself as a significant professional activity.

The sample essay 'Justifying English language teaching' could be photocopied and used in a number of ways:

(a) Students could study it as homework in preparation for the next task (this is recommended only for very weak groups).

(b) Students could be given the essay *after* Task 2, Step 2 (i.e. after planning).

(c) Students could be given the essay *after* Task 2, Step 3 (i.e. after writing and evaluating the first draft).

(d) Students could be given the essay *after* Task 2, Step 4 (i.e. after the peer evaluation of the first draft).

Your choice will depend on the needs and level of the group. Option (b) may be appropriate for relatively weak groups. Options (c) and (d) will reduce the likelihood of imitation in students' drafts and more proficient groups will benefit from this. You could even opt to give out the sample essay after students have completed their second drafts, if they seem especially able.

In any event, the essay provides a useful example of justification for those students who are less familiar with it. Whenever you give it out, it would be useful to go through it carefully with the students, especially in terms of its structure.

1. Ask students to analyse the sample essay paragraph by paragraph, and build up a plan on the board as follows:

Paragraph	Content
1	Definition of subject Unorthodox ideas
2	Challenging assumptions
3	Vested interests
4	Economic factors
5	Contributions to the world

2. Discuss the linkage between paragraphs. Also note the use of the following:

It must be acknowledged that …
As far as X is/are concerned …
Although it could be argued that …

These are impersonal ways of making a point. In Unit 7, there will be an opportunity to show how a writer can either display or avoid commitment when writing.

3. Discuss any other issues or points of clarification which arise.

Step 1

Discussion of audience and context for publication or presentation can either be in pairs or in plenary. Try to ensure that students make appropriate and workable choices and maintain these choices consistently in the way in which their essays are organised and written.

2.1   Refer students again to the points on the question sheet on page 44 of the Student's Book and ask them to apply the points to their own subject or profession. Elicit questions and respond to them, particularly if some students still seem unsure about how these can be applied.

2.2   Refer students to the pre-writing questions in 2.2 of the Student's Book.

2.3   Circulate and monitor the discussion. Intervene and answer questions, offering guidance when necessary.

 Step 2

2.4, 2.5   Circulate and oversee students' planning. Offer guidance if and when you think it necessary. Some of the planning has already been carried out in Task 1. Make sure that students are aware of this and do not make more work for themselves than is necessary.

2.6   Circulate and monitor the discussion and peer evaluation of plans. Answer questions, prompting and offering guidance as necessary. By this stage students should be reasonably efficient in evaluating organisation.

2.7   Continue circulating and engage in individual discussion to ascertain whether or not each student has treated his or her partner's comments critically. Make sure that misguided advice does not lead to extraneous problems in otherwise adequate plans.

 Step 3

2.8   Ask students to begin writing their first draft. As they write, circulate, prompting and intervening where necessary. Remind students when they have finished their first drafts to indicate at the top of the first page the choices they have made about readership and context for presentation.

2.9, 2.10   After they have finished writing, ask students to carry out a preliminary evaluation of their own drafts with the aid of the post-writing question in 2.9 of the Student's Book and the specified sections of Evaluation Checklists A and B. Encourage them not to consult with each other at this stage so that they don't become too dependent on a partner's advice. Circulate and assist as necessary. If students seem to need or want assistance at this stage, read through parts of completed drafts and encourage them to discuss some of their own preliminary evaluation with you.

Supplementary exercise

The following exercise may be helpful, especially with less proficient groups. Before Step 4, collect first drafts and chose one draft as the 'focus' draft for general discussion. Put it on a xerox or overhead transparency or make one paper copy per student. An overhead transparency is preferable because it can then produce a focus for general discussion.

Your choice of essay will depend on your view of the dynamics of the class and on the quality of the essays. It's probably best to choose one that is not perfect (because there will be little to say about it) but is not a total disaster either.

1. Display the 'focus' draft on the overhead projector and read through it with the students. Make cosmetic corrections as you read, but don't draw attention to these.

2. Ask students to suggest higher level improvements, such as features of organisation, improved ways of introducing or concluding, and places where information could be added.

3. Go through the essay paragraph by paragraph, eliciting specific improvements. Where necessary, make suggestions of your own. Incorporate the improvements on an overlay so that you can tinker around without changing the original.

4. Sum up the changes which have been made and give students time to make parallel improvements to their own draft. Circulate around the class, intervening where necessary or answering questions. Make sure that all students have made some improvements.

 Step 4

2.11 Ask students to exchange drafts and read them carefully.

2.12 After students have read their partner's draft, ask them to apply the post-writing question in 2.9 of the Student's Book. Whether the students use Evaluation Checklist A or B will depend on a number of factors, such as the level and needs of the group, your own preference and the students' preferences. Evaluation Checklist A may be more suitable for less proficient groups. Again, a selective use of the evaluation checklist is advisable here. Both checklists will be consulted again in Step 5, with a different emphasis for each one.

2.13 Ask students to apply the points in the specific sections of Evaluation Checklist A or B.

2.14 Again stress the importance of making detailed written comments, either on their partner's draft or on another piece of paper. If some students would prefer to do this after the discussion, this is acceptable as long as the written comments are made in detail.

2.15 Circulate and monitor the process of discussion. Answer questions and deal with problems, as necessary. To provide additional help, especially with weaker groups, you may want to summarise in plenary the main points that have emerged from their discussions with each other. If there are problems which most students are experiencing, deal with them on the board or overhead projector.

As in Step 2.7, ask students individually how they have evaluated their partner's comments and for what reasons. If the class is large and time is limited, a possible approach is to ask each student to describe in detail *one* comment with which he or she disagrees and to say why. Resolution of one point may enable this student to deal with other points more confidently.

 Step 5

2.16 After the peer evaluation has been completed, encourage students to continue to work on their drafts before they rewrite. Circulate and offer guidance with the use of either of the evaluation checklists if needed. The sections specified in the Student's Book (Sections 5 and 6 of Evaluation Checklist A and Sections 4 and 6 of Evaluation Checklist B) provide further guidelines which complement those already used in Steps 3 and 4.

For more ambitious students who are reasonably confident about their knowledge and use of grammar, you may want to include Section 5 of Evaluation Checklist B in this final self-evaluation.

2.17 The final draft will probably be produced as homework, as in previous units, unless you feel that further monitoring is necessary. Collect all the drafts, and, as before, emphasise that they should hand in all the written stages of their writing process: brainstorming, plans, first drafts and final drafts. You may want to stress again to students that only the final draft will be marked.

Conclude by asking students to summarise what they have learnt in this unit. You may want to refer back to the texts in Reading Unit 5 to stimulate discussion. It may be interesting to elicit discussion of how helpful they feel this unit has been in relation to the work they are doing in the Study Skill sessions.

If you find too little evidence of evaluation and development from one stage to another in an essay, an individual conference with the student concerned may be advisable. By the end of this unit students should be reasonably confident and efficient in both self-evaluation and peer evaluation.

Answers to the question sheet

Here are some answers to the question sheet on page 44 of the Students' Book. You will want to suggest other answers yourself.

1. The body of knowledge in ELT is concerned with the structure of English; the ways in which languages are learnt; ways of designing courses and teaching materials; methods of teaching; and forms of evaluation. Although ELT is influenced by a wide range of theory and research, some methods, such as community language learning, suggestopaedia and 'The Silent Way' have not achieved widespread acceptance because they do not fit in with mainstream theory and methodology.

2. Sometimes specialists in other fields, such as education, and organisations which sponsor students, may challenge the assumptions of ELT but, on the whole, very few people have the opportunity to question our assumptions.

3. There is an exclusive community of scholars whose interests are served by ELT. In addition, ELT is a very large service industry, worth about £1 billion per year to the UK, which involves British foreign policy (via the British Council and Overseas Development Authority), universities, colleges, private language schools, publishers of ELT textbooks, and the tourist industry.

4. There is a close relationship between ELT and vested interests. For instance, publishers depend on new ideas and new writers to produce more and more material for an expanding ELT market both in the UK and overseas. These ideas and writers come from universities, colleges and language schools. In turn, these organisations buy the materials which the publishers produce.

5. The ordinary citizen in some parts of the UK comes into contact with overseas students who have come to this country to learn English, and so the local economy can benefit from their presence here. Overseas, children will probably be learning English at school, and learning English has become an increasingly important job requirement in many countries, notably continental Europe. All these people can benefit from the improved methods and materials developed by ELT specialists. At the same time, people will find it difficult to have access to the learning of English except through institutional structures and published materials.

6. ELT affects my own community indirectly by providing the basis of a large service industry. Internationally, ELT supports a worldwide network of teaching which is contributing to the growth of English as an international language, so that people virtually everywhere in the world are influenced by my subject. ELT also contributes to the hegemony of knowledge by the developed world because underdeveloped countries have to put scarce resources into ELT so as to ensure that they can gain access to knowledge through English. (It could be argued that they would have to put resources into translating such information into the vernacular(s) anyway.)

UNIT 6 INTERNATIONAL TOURISM

TASK 1

Task 1 can be approached in various ways, according to the needs and level of the group. In many countries, participating in external tourism is not yet affordable. In others, tourism is perceived as a necessary and/or desirable source of income. Some have no influx of foreign tourism, while others regulate it carefully.

Some students may need input from the texts before they have enough understanding of tourism from a Western point of view to write an extended definition of tourism. If so, Route B or C is recommended rather than Route A.

Route A
Complete Task 1 as set out below, before going on to the texts in Task 2.

Route B
Task 1 after Text 6.2
or Task 1, Step 1; then Texts 6.1 and 6.2; then Task 1, Step 2.

Route C
Task 1 after Text 6.4
or Task 1, Step 1; then Texts 6.1–6.4; then Task 1, Step 2.

 Step 1

1.1 If the students are studying in a foreign country, they will almost certainly be tourists from time to time. Use the questions to elicit group discussion of tourism.

1.2 Ask students to write a formal definition of tourism. (Remind them of work done in Reading Units 4 and 5, and in Writing Unit 5.)

Concept	is	Class	which	Special feature(s)
		a form of ...	where	
		a type of ...	who	
		the practice of ...	that	
		the business of ...		

Example:

Tourism is: 1. the practice of travelling for pleasure, especially on one's holidays.
2. the business of providing holidays, tours, hotels, etc. for tourists.

Step 2

1.3 Ask students to extend their definitions by discussing three or more of the questions in 1.3 of the Student's Book.

Ask them to write an extended definition which includes three or four extra pieces of information from the discussion based on these questions.

TASK 2

From the discussion it may have emerged that tourism can create problems and not everyone is in favour of it. Refer students to the opening paragraphs of Text 6.1 on page 46 of the Student's Book.

Text 6.1

2.1 Ask students to:

- describe the problem identified by the writer
- summarise Text 6.1 using no more than two sentences.

The first sentence could form one part of the summary, while the narrative part could be summarised along the following lines:

Annoyed by the repeated noise from an open-top tourist bus, they drenched the tourists with the full blast from a hosepipe.

or *They drenched the tourists on an open-top tourist bus which repeatedly disturbed their peace and quiet.*

Note that this sentence could be linked to the first one by *when*:

when, annoyed by ...
when they drenched ...

It would be helpful to explain the ironic reformulation in the title of the postcard cliché 'Wish you were here'. Text 6.3 has a similarly ironic title.

Text 6.2

The writer goes on to present information to illustrate the scale of the problem, and he notes the apparent lack of government concern.

2.2 Ask students to read the text and to describe the *function* of the text – what the writer is trying to make clear to the reader.

You may want to introduce students to or remind them of the function of exemplification here, although the characteristic markers are not used. Note also the exercises on the second paragraph of Text 6.4.

Elicit the contrast between past and present in the opening paragraph. The use of the simple past and present/present perfect infinitive and the time indicator **In the last couple of years** signal this. Ask students why the writer has chosen to use such a contrast at this point in the text – what it contributes in terms of interest and emphasis. The needs of readers in a journalistic context are relevant here.

2.3 Ask students to summarise Text 6.2 using no more than three sentences.

2.4 Ask students to consider what the writer's attitude is towards tourism, and how this attitude is revealed in the article as a whole (Texts 6.1 and 6.2). Note words and phrases like:

Text 6.1: (a) **War had been declared**
Text 6.2: (b) **an uncontrolled flood**
         (c) **summer battlegrounds**
         (d) **vast armies**
         (e) **fortified with burgers**
         (f) **a takeaway piece of British Heritage**
         (g) **the Government apparently … blind eye**
         (h) **the British Government avoids**

With advanced groups, it may be useful to point out the writer's craftsmanship in his cleverly sustained patterns of exaggerated images:

- (a), (c), (d) and (e), and less directly (g), all involve military metaphors/ personification.
- (e) and (f) involve fast-food metaphors.

His language is unusually figurative for a journalistic text. *Metaphor, personification* and *hyperbole* may be helpful terms here.

The humorous and ironic tone of some parts of this article is sometimes difficult for students to gauge because the issues are at the same time treated seriously. The title provides a signal of the irony to come. It could be pointed out that articles in the 'quality' newspapers often contain a mixture of registers and tones like this.

Text 6.3

2.5 Ask students to read Text 6.3 and identify the topic in each paragraph.

- Paragraph 1: The historical growth in tourism
- Paragraph 2: The unsatisfied appetite for travel
- Paragraph 3: Projected growth leads to problems.

You may want to point out the narrative use of time here. Ask students:

- how many time periods are specified in the opening paragraph
- how these are established through:
  - time indicators, dates and historical references (you may need to explain **The Romans**)
  - verb tenses:
    The Romans had …
    went … in 1096
    Before 1939 … travelled
    Now, after three decades … are …

Remind students that a chronological order is not the only order used by writers in narrative texts, whether fictional or non-fictional. Provide examples of this if you wish.

2.6 Ask students to summarise the text using no more than three sentences. Refer them to the main ideas already identified.

Supplementary exercise 1

This exercise can be omitted if you wish.

Refer back to Text 6.3 and ask students to identify the occurrences of *could*. What does this verb tell us about the statement which the writer is making? Why does the writer show some uncertainty in these statements?

Ask students to compare statements of certainty in Text 6.3 with statements of uncertainty.

Certain	Uncertain/possible
There are more than 400 million a year.	There could be up to 650 million.
These are mass movements without parallel in history.	
Many analysts cannot credit them.	
The population swells by 100 million tourists each year.	UN projections say visitors could number 760 million by 2025.
	X has hinted at the prospect of air traffic being 'capped'.
The only certainties for the traveller are delays and congestion.	

Then ask students to consider the following:

- What could happen if the number of Japanese tourists doubles?
- What could happen if more tourists come from the Pacific Rim countries?

- What could happen if there is too much air traffic?
- What could happen to tourist attractions which are too popular?

Text 6.4

One of the advantages of tourism is the economic benefits it brings to places and people. Ask students to:

- discuss examples of the economic benefits of tourism
- consider who actually benefits.

Then ask them to read Text 6.4.

2.7 Ask students to identify the main idea in each paragraph. As it happens, the main point of the text is stated in the three opening sentences of the first paragraph (the first is effectively the topic sentence).

2.8 Discuss the function of the second paragraph in relation to the first. Elicit/ introduce the term *exemplification* here. (Refer to Text 6.2, especially the second paragraph.)
Point out the words **examples** and **illustrate** and discuss other forms of the language of exemplification.

2.9 Ask students to summarise the text using no more than two sentences. Establish the point that a summary doesn't have to include the fine detail of the examples in paragraph 2.

Texts 6.5 and 6.6

Ask students to consider what solution could be found to the problem of tourism and its effect on the places tourists visit and the people who live there. Then ask students to read and discuss Texts 6.5 and 6.6, which present different solutions to this problem.

2.10 Ask students to say which parts of Texts 6.5 and 6.6 deal with:

- situation
- problem
- solution
- evaluation/comment.

Text 6.5 presents one solution to the (implied) problem. Text 6.6 presents others. The organisation of Text 6.6 can be outlined as:

- Paragraph 1:   Situation   or   Solution
- Paragraph 2:   Problem   Further problem
- Paragraph 3:   Solution + evaluation   Further solution + evaluation

Supplementary exercise 2

Refer students back to the questions which they discussed in 1.3. Do they now have fuller answers to any of the questions?

To conclude, ask students to re-read Texts 6.1–6.6 in preparation for the writing task in Task 3, in which the topic will be:

> **Tourism: what can be done?**

Very proficient groups could compare and contrast the overall approach and use of language in Barrett's (B) and Nicholson-Lord's (NL) articles (Texts 6.1–6.2 and Texts 6.3–6.6 respectively). The differences could be described in these terms:

1. A relative absence of figurative language in NL and a more discursive approach. Highly figurative language in B and a more imaginative, provocative approach.
2. Fuller use of supporting evidence and statistics in NL.
3. A wider overview in NL, including the history of world tourism and future prospects. B concentrates more on the UK.
4. A more formal, impersonal, 'sober' style in NL. A more informal, individual and 'colourful' style in B.
5. Similar ironic reformuation of clichés in the titles of both B and NL.

Specific features could be extracted from the texts and used to support each point.

TASK 3

By now you will have covered the following:

- definition of tourism
- statements of problems
- suggested solutions.

The next step is to ask students to write a complete essay which defines the topic, presents the problems and argues for a solution or solutions.

As before, ask students to think about both the audience/readership and context for publication/presentation of their writing before they begin.

Remind students that they have already written an essay in Unit 4 involving the **Situation→Problem→Solution→Evaluation** pattern of organisation. This essay has a different emphasis but will give them further practice in developing the pattern.

 Step 1

3.1 Refer students again to the texts in Task 2, which they should have reviewed in preparation for this task. Point out that these texts can be useful sources of evidence for their essays. Refer them also to Text 6.7 on page 53 of the Student's Book, which summarises tourism's global impact. Students can use some of this information in their essays.

3.2 The five pre-writing questions in 3.2 of the Student's Book will help students think about the implications of their readership in relation to the content of their essays. Circulate and monitor the discussion if you opt for pair work here. Plenary discussion can follow this.

Some students may come from countries which will never attract tourists. What position can they take on tourism and its effects on people and the environment? What lessons can they learn from the effects of tourism elsewhere? Other students may come from countries where tourism is still perceived as necessary and/or desirable. They may be able to write about possible future problems and solutions.

Sample essay

The following essay on tourism can be photocopied and used in one of several ways which are outlined below the text.

Tourism

Tourism is defined by the *Longman Dictionary of Contemporary English* as the practice of travelling for pleasure, especially on one's holidays and the business of providing holiday tours, hotels, etc. for tourists. There are many forms of tourism, including economical package tours to popular holiday resorts, individual travel by independent tourists and exclusive, luxurious arrangements for the rich.

Tourism has a long history, and the First Crusade in the 11th century is an early version of the package tour. Medieval or modern, tourism is associated with a wide range of service industries which provide transport, accommodation, catering, shopping and entertainment. In Britain alone, tourism has contributed around 1.5 million jobs and more than £14 billion to the economy (Nicholson-Lord 1990:5).

Unfortunately, the success of tourism in Britain has led to problems of overcrowding and 'tourist pollution' (Barrett 1990). In the first five months of 1990, there was an increase of 6 per cent in overseas visitors to Britain, while in the past 12 months, 17.5 million visitors came to this country. Other popular tourist places are also receiving huge numbers of visitors. For instance, the population of the Mediterranean coastline increases from 130 to 230 million annually.

Such large numbers of tourists have considerable economic, environmental and social effects. In the Mediterranean, tourism is a principal cause of pollution, while in the Caribbean 90 per cent of waste is dumped into the sea. The resulting pollution is destroying mangrove forests, seagrass beds and coral reefs. Tourist developments and holiday resorts are leading to urbanisation. This is particularly bad in Spain, France, Italy and Greece where 95 per cent of the coast could be urbanised by 2025 (Nicholson-Lord 1990:3).

Although tourism is claimed to produce considerable economic advantages, it is not always the local people who benefit. In the Pacific, three-quarters of the revenue goes to the multinational tour operators. In Goa, hotels get piped water while villagers go without. In the third world, tourism can lead to a 'one-crop' economy, dependent on the 'whims of Western consumer fashion and the financial dictates of the tour operators' (Nicholson-Lord 1990:5).

This growing problem requires a solution before tourism destroys the planet. One solution is the development of so-called 'Green Tourism', which is small-scale, makes use of existing resources and attempts to bring tourists into closer contact with the host culture and society. However, Green Tourism is a limited solution to a global problem. Another solution is to put tourists into holiday ghettos, isolated from the local community. Many holiday-makers are happy with such an arrangement.

A third solution was suggested by Sir Edmund Hillary, speaking at a tourism seminar in Osaka. 'Don't go around the world clustered together in great bus-loads,' he said. 'Go in twos or threes or fours and you will enjoy it much more and find yourselves much more welcome.' (Jenkins 1990:18).

It is clear that tourism must be controlled, otherwise the things and places which tourists go to see and visit will be destroyed. New forms of tourism which are less destructive can be developed, while alternative and more varied forms of economic development can be encouraged so as to reduce the dependence of third world countries on the one-crop economy of tourism.

References

Barrett, F. (1990) 'Wish you weren't here', *The Independent*, 15 August 1990
Jenkins, R. (1990) 'The pros and cons of tourism', *The Independent Magazine*, 7 April 1990
Nicholson-Lord, D. (1990) 'Death by tourism', *The Independent on Sunday* (supplement), 5 August 1990

Uses for the essay

1. The essay could be referred to as a guide (rather than a model) at different stages in the session. For example, in the work on writing an extended definition (especially with less proficient groups), reference could be made to the first two paragraphs, and alternative ways of writing the definition could be explored. You will find that we have only included information in answer to some of the questions given in 1.3, so there is still plenty of room for variation in the kinds of things which are included in the extended definition. Much will depend on what has emerged in the class discussion.

2. The essay could be introduced and discussed before the planning stage, after the planning stage or even after the first draft. The two latter options will reduce the likelihood of imitation. With weaker groups, however, it may be better to introduce and discuss the essay relatively early. If so, option (c) or (d) could be considered.

3. At some stage in the unit the essay could be evaluated and improved. New information and ideas could be substituted or added. For example, a more specific title could be added. Also, there will be ideas that the students themselves have produced which could be used.

4. A more forceful conclusion could be substituted for the one given. Hopefully, the discussion will become politicised and controversial and the conclusion could be made much more radical than the one provided.

 Step 2

3.3 Ask students to brainstorm. Remind them again of the importance of using rough notes rather than complete sentences. Set a time limit if you think this will help to achieve spontaneity and speed. If they have reviewed the six texts in Task 2, they should be ready with ideas.

3.4 Ask students to begin planning their essay by developing and rearranging the results of their brainstorming session. Draw their attention to the guidelines in 3.4, which should help them to formulate a more effective plan. If they wish, they can use the outline given below and on page 51 of the Students' Book to help them in their planning. Emphasise, however, that they do not have to follow the suggested outline exactly. It is only given as an example.

Supplementary exercise 3

If you find that students have problems with planning the essay at this point, the following exercise may be helpful before 3.5.

Discuss in plenary what ideas could go into each section of the essay, drawing on the material covered in earlier activities. It may be helpful to make notes on the board or overhead projector.

Organisation of essay	
Definition:	What is tourism?
Situation:	What is the present situation regarding tourism?
	How did it come about?
	What are the main features of the situation?
Problem:	Is there a problem? If so, what is it?
Solution/ Response:	How can the problem be dealt with?
	What alternative solutions are there?
	What constraints are there on each possible solution?
Evaluation:	Which of the solutions is likely to be the most effective?
	What would be the result of applying each of the solutions?

In addition, ask students to relate the problem to their own experience or situation.

Students should now be able to organise their essays, following the outline given above if they wish, and incorporating more examples of their own. Remind them to justify their suggestions for a solution and give specific examples or evidence in support of them.

3.5 Circulate and prompt where you feel it is needed.

3.6 Continue circulating and engage in individual discussion to ascertain whether or not each student has treated his or her partner's comments critically. Make sure that misguided advice does not lead to extraneous problems in otherwise adequate plans.

At this stage you may want to remind students of the conventions of referencing and quotation by referring them to the sample essay on tourism and eliciting examples to be written on the board or overhead projector. Point out that this ties in with what they have learned or are learning if they are using the Study Skills book in this series.

 Step 3

Suggest that students begin their essays in an interesting and provocative way and that they end in a way which brings the reader back to the beginning.

3.7 Ask them to begin writing their first draft. As they write, circulate and intervene where necessary. Question and prompt if they seem to want your help.

3.8 After they have finished writing, ask students to carry out a preliminary evaluation of their own drafts with the aid of the six post-writing questions in 3.8 of the Student's Book. Encourage them not to consult with each other at this stage so that they don't become too dependent on a partner's advice. Circulate and assist as necessary. If students seem to need or want assistance at this stage, read through parts of completed drafts and encourage them to discuss some of their preliminary evaluations with you.

 Step 4

3.9 Ask students to exchange drafts and to read their partner's draft carefully.

3.10 After students have read their partner's draft, ask them to apply the post-writing questions in 3.8 of the Student's Book.

3.11 Ask students to apply the points in the specified sections of either Evaluation Checklist A or B.

By this stage students should be reasonably familiar with both evaluation checklists. You may prefer to focus on sections other than the ones suggested here. Most of the post-writing questions focus on content, and for this reason the sections in Evaluation Checklists A and B on organisation/cohesion have been highlighted at this point.

3.12 Again stress the importance of making detailed written comments, either on their partner's draft or on another piece of paper. If some students would prefer to do this after the discussion, this is acceptable as long as the written comments are made in detail.

3.13 Circulate and monitor the process of discussion. Answer questions and deal with problems, as necessary. To provide additional help, especially to weaker groups, you may want to summarise in plenary the main points that have emerged from their discussions with each other. If there are problems which most students are experiencing, deal with them on the board or overhead projector.

As in 3.6, ask students individually how they have evaluated their partner's comments and for what reasons. If the class is large and time is limited, a possible approach is to ask each student to describe in detail one comment with which he or she disagrees and to say why. Resolution of one point may enable this student to deal with other points more confidently.

 Step 5

3.14 After the peer evaluation has been completed, encourage students to continue to work on their drafts before they rewrite. Circulate and offer guidance with the use of either of the evaluation checklists if necessary. Sections 5 and 6 of Evaluation Checklist A and Sections 4 and 6 of Evaluation Checklist B provide further guidelines which complement those already used in Steps 3 and 4.

For more ambitious students who are reasonably confident about their knowledge and use of grammar, you may want to include Section 5 of Evaluation Checklist B in this final self-evaluation.

3.15 The final draft will probably be produced as homework, as in previous units, unless you feel that further monitoring is necessary.

Discussion

The relation between the topics in Reading Unit 6 and Writing Unit 6 was highlighted at the beginning of this unit. You may want to ask students how and why the changes in international diplomacy and in international tourism are related. It may be useful to focus on the causes of change in each area; for example, the media and telecommunications.

If you find too little evidence of evaluation and development from one stage to another in an essay, an individual conference with the student concerned may be advisable. By the end of this unit students should be reasonably confident and efficient in both self-evaluation and peer evaluation.

UNIT 7

INTERNATIONAL STUDENTS

INTRODUCTION

This unit is a culmination of work done in the previous units, notably Unit 2, and it is intended to increase students' ability to develop and write an argument incorporating statistical data and acknowledging the sources of the data. The distinction between impersonal and personal styles of argument is also highlighted, linked to ways of showing accountability on the part of the writer. It is also intended to provide practice in writing a conclusion which draws together the main argument convincingly.

The issue of the way in which writers accept accountability for their arguments is an increasingly important one. Although, conventionally, academic writing is impersonal in style as a way of promoting objectivity, in many disciplines, particularly in the social sciences and humanities, this style is losing ground to a more personal and engaged style. An important indicator of this change lies in the increasing use of the first person singular pronoun. The issue is introduced in Tasks 4–5 of this unit to raise students' awareness and give them an opportunity to experiment with the use of a more personal, yet academic, style of argument.

The topic that has been chosen is one that should be close to the students' hearts: students studying outside their own country. For the purposes of this unit, Britain is used as an example, but other destinations or host countries can be substituted if you have access to relevant information.

This unit provides statistical information from national sources as well as data from university sources, and includes a series of activities to help students analyse and make sense of the tables. In this way, students should be able to take relevant information from the tables to incorporate in their own writing. They should also acknowledge the source of the information along the lines shown in the tables themselves because, of course, the credibility of such data depends on being able to judge the reliability of the source.

The whole unit should take about a week to complete, so try to pace it accordingly. By now you will have a good idea of how long things take with your class and so you should be able to judge how many sessions you will require to cover this unit and how much writing will be done in class and for homework.

Work through Tasks 1 and 2 in whatever way you find most appropriate and productive with your class. You may wish to deal with the activities in plenary or you may prefer to split the class into small groups (no more than four students per group). If you do work in groups, it will be necessary to summarise the outcome of each activity in plenary.

It may also be judged appropriate, at some point, to tell students that current UK government policy is to encourage UK universities to recruit international students to offset the economic constraints which they are facing. UK universities are being encouraged to increase student intake without any additional funding. The differential between home and international student fees is not, in itself, a recent phenomenon (it was actually introduced in 1968 by a Labour government but the present Conservative government has, by its policies, virtually forced universities to increase the differential and to charge international students whatever 'the market can bear').

Paradoxically, a significant number of international students receive aid scholarships (as shown in Table 7.2 on page 57 of the Student's Book), so in effect government money is going from the Treasury via the Overseas Development Administration and the British Council to the universities! Whether or not you want to open the discussion up to the economics and politics of this is up to you. It could be time-consuming and rather complicated.

Organisation of Unit 7

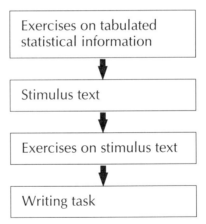

```
┌─────────────────────────────┐
│ Exercises on tabulated      │
│ statistical information     │
└─────────────────────────────┘
              │
              ▼
┌─────────────────────────────┐
│ Stimulus text               │
└─────────────────────────────┘
              │
              ▼
┌─────────────────────────────┐
│ Exercises on stimulus text  │
└─────────────────────────────┘
              │
              ▼
┌─────────────────────────────┐
│ Writing task                │
└─────────────────────────────┘
```

TASK 1

 Step 1

1.1 Tables 7.1 and 7.2 are taken from the annual statistics prepared by the Overseas Relations Unit of a British university (here called 'Redlands'). The purpose of 1.1 is to 'read' the statistics as a step in the process of obtaining and interpreting information for the writing activity later in the unit.

Step 2

1.2 From the figures in Table 2, we can assume that the majority of overseas post-graduates are sponsored by agencies rather than family money.

1.3 Encourage students to reflect on the trends in Tables 7.1 and 7.2 from their own viewpoint. The figures show that overseas students represent a significant part of the student body at Redlands University. In short, such students are a significant resource.

TASK 2

 Step 1

This task will require interpretation of the tables and some arithmetic.

2.1 There are 756 postgraduate students from developing countries. Thus, according to our calculations the sum is as follows:

$$£5000 \times 756 = £3,780,000$$

This is a considerable sum of money and you might like to consider in discussion with the students how significant this sum is as a contribution to the income of Redlands University. It is important to focus on the source of funding for students from developing countries and to discuss the significance of this.

2.2 The sum is as follows:

Total expenditure on goods & services = £5,000 × £1.17 × No. of students
= £5,000 × £1.17 × 756
= £4,422,600

Again, this is a large sum. This is the amount which students would have to pay in fees for hall of residence or other accommodation fees, food, clothing, transport, entertainment and so on. Most of this would go into the local economy.

2.3 The questions in the Student's Book are intended to stimulate discussion on the significance of this income from international students for the local economy.

2.4 This paragraph can be both descriptive and predictive. Students could be encouraged to consider what could happen if international student numbers decline rather than remain stable or rise.

TASK 3

This particular task involves the transition from the data base, as it were, to the argument.

Step 1

3.1 Before reading Text 7.1, use the questions in 3.1 to discuss attitudes to foreign workers and students. In some countries, there are not many foreign students, but there may be a large number of foreign workers. Attitudes to such people may range from highly favourable to grossly prejudiced. Clearly, this can be a very controversial topic, as it could lead to a parade of prejudices (on both sides), so your role as chairperson is important. Try to encourage students to distinguish between objective information and expressions of opinion. If there is little or no discussion, you may have to stimulate it by referring to locally available statistics or expressions of concern or prejudice in the local media.

 Step 2

3.2 After the discussion, turn to the letter (Text 7.1). You can either read it aloud to the students or leave them to read it silently and individually, or, if there is a good reader in the class, you could ask him or her to read it to the class. Do whatever you think will work best and then encourage post-reading discussion in 3.3.

Note: As in the letter in Unit 2, the name and address of the correspondent has been withheld, although it was supplied to the editor of the newspaper. Point out that newspapers and magazines will not usually accept a letter for publication without having the writer's name and address. Giving one's name and address is a sign of good faith – or of being accountable for what one says.

3.3 One of the aims here is to distinguish between what is understandable and what is reasonable. It may be quite understandable that the correspondent has the views he expresses – there may be personal reasons why he feels like this – but is it reasonable for him to have and express these views? And does he provide a reasoned or justified argument to support them?

No doubt some students will feel very strongly about the correspondent's views – or about attitudes towards themselves as foreign students which they have detected among people they have encountered abroad during their studies, such as hall of residence staff, shop-keepers, and members of the public in general. If they do feel strongly, all the better, because it will help you to get across to them the distinction between personal/subjective argument and impersonal/objective argument, and the stylistic features of each.

3.4 Ask students to summarise the arguments in no more than four sentences.

TASK 4

Point out that in an English-speaking academic culture, people engaged in academic argument try to separate the argument from the person who is arguing, and that it is common for people to argue on opposite sides in a very committed and engaged fashion, yet still to remain personal friends. In other words, there is role separation between that of academic advocate and that of personal colleague or friend.

In some cultures, such a separation of the individual from the argument is not usual, so if A argues against B's argument, B will take this personally and may then consider A to be his or her 'enemy'. This can happen in an English-speaking culture too, of course, but it is less common in professional and academic contexts where people will play devil's advocate as a means of thoroughly analysing a case for and against something.

It is important for students to realise that if someone criticises their argument or what they have written, this doesn't mean that they are being criticised personally. It is also possible to be criticised as a person (for rude behaviour, sloppiness, carelessness, etc.) but to be valued as a student, researcher, colleague or teacher.

So, try to get across the point that academic writing usually has an impersonal/ objectives style (even if there is a very strong personal commitment to the viewpoint being argued) and that a failure to adopt and maintain this style of argument can lead to a communication breakdown because academic readers will expect such a style. Arguing personally can result in the academic reader rejecting the argument – even if the argument is a good one.

 Step 1

4.1 This should generate some interesting discussion and highlight a range of cultural attitudes and practices concerning the uses of argument in writing and speaking. In some cultures, for example, it is considered impolite to refer to oneself as an individual in most contexts (*we* is the polite pronoun). In others, personal forms of argument are very rare and only used in situations of serious aggression. It may be useful to contrast impersonal forms of argument with, say, the forms of argument that might be used among friends in a pub or similar informal setting in Britain.

 Step 2

4.2 Remind students of the work they did in Unit 2. Make sure that they summarise and discuss the ways in which a writer achieves an impersonal/objective style by referring to specific points in Text 7.2. It is a good idea to make students focus on specific items and list them. If they don't, they may not see the point(s) or may be unable to take them in properly.

4.3 Suggest that students make lists of items from Text 7.1 in the left-hand column and corresponding items from Text 7.2 in the right-hand column in their tables. This should lead to a more thorough and concentrated focus. Students can work in groups, with each group working on one of the four paragraphs.

If students have initial problems with this activity, compare the first paragraphs in plenary on the board or overhead projector. Then see if they can continue working in pairs.

4.4

Showing commitment (Text 7.1)	Hedging (Text 7.2)
I think this is wrong	It could be argued that …
We should give priority	It seems that …
I think the government is wrong	It could be asked what …
They should stay in their own countries	It appears that …

Steps 1 and 2 are intended to help students see the stylistic difference between a personal argument (represented by Text 7.1) and an academic style of argument (represented by Text 7.2). Deal with the contrast in whatever way you feel will best help students to see the point.

Again, remind the students of the two versions of the 'letter to the editor' they studied in Unit 2.

TASK 5

 Step 1

In this activity, students are asked to choose the most effective concluding paragraph and to explain the reasons for their choice. This should help them to apply the 'input' about conclusions.

5.1 The original conclusion was number 3. It would help to explain why the other four are not suitable or less suitable – for example, the first merely repeats the introductory paragraph.

 Step 2

5.2 These questions may become superfluous if the discussion in Step 1 elicits these points fully. If not, they may help to clarify further the effectiveness of the conclusion in relation to the thesis.

5.3 This activity focuses on the ways in which the writer hedges, developing the point introduced in Task 4. Ways in which the writer hedges include the use of:

- modal verbs: **could be concluded/argued that, would be, can be concluded**
- adverb indicating attitude: **undoubtedly**.

 Step 3

5.5 Text 7.3 embodies a mixture of personal and impersonal styles which is increasingly typical of academic writing. Part of the effectiveness of an argument derives from the extent to which the writer is prepared to be accountable for the points he or she makes. In Text 7.3, the writer displays accountability through the use of the following phrases:

I would like to argue that …   **I believe that …**
It seems to me that …   **I wish to advocate …**
In my view …

The use of the first person shows clearly that the writer is responsible for the points being made. The writer also uses polite ways of telling the reader how he or she is going to proceed:

I would like to argue …   **I wish to advocate …**

The policy advocated in the final paragraph is also tentative:

[it] would benefit this country …

If the writer had wished to be make a stronger statement, he or she would have used *will* (**[it] will benefit this country**).

TASK 6

In this task, unlike most of the previous tasks, the audience, context and purpose for writing are already specified for students. It is helpful for them to have to make fewer decisions at this stage because they will have to consolidate several new skills in writing this essay.

In this task students contribute a short paper to an imaginary collection of papers. The strength of their argument will be increased if they use statistical information, such as that displayed in Tables 1 to 4 in this unit. Ways of referring to tabulated information appear in Appendix 3.

 Step 1

6.1 In addition to statistical information on numbers, fees paid and so on, encourage students to consider factors such as:

- the contribution of international research students to research in their field
- the contribution of international research students to existing research projects (it is common in science and technology for graduate students to be directed to work that fits in with departmental or professorial research projects)
- the contribution to internationalism
- the political benefits of having tomorrow's decision-makers study in the UK or the host country where they are studying.

6.2 Note, too, that it is important to observe the conventions of citing sources. Ask students to consider why it is important to cite sources. Refer to Unit 6.

Step 2

6.3 Ask students to begin planning their essay by developing and rearranging what they brainstormed in Step 1. Draw their attention to the points listed in 6.3 of the Student's Book, which should help them to formulate a more effective plan.

6.4 Circulate and prompt where you feel it is needed. If serious problems with organisation are evident, you may want to put the sample plan below on the board or overhead projector.

Sample plan

Paragraph	Content/purpose
1	Outline of paper
2	Thesis
3	Supporting idea Evidence
4	Supporting idea Evidence
5	Conclusion: reference back to thesis and concluding statement wrapping up the argument

6.5 Continue circulating and engage in individual discussion to ascertain whether the students have treated their partners' comments critically. Make sure that misguided advice does not lead to extraneous problems in otherwise adequate plans.

 Step 3

Suggest that students begin their papers in an interesting and provocative way and that they end in a way which brings the reader back to the beginning. Remind students of the work done on conclusions in Task 5 of this unit.

6.6 Ask them to begin writing their first draft. As they write, circulate and intervene where necessary. Question and prompt the students if they seem to want your help.

6.7 After they have finished writing, ask students to carry out a preliminary evaluation of their own drafts with the aid of the post-writing questions in 6.7 of the Student's Book. Encourage them not to consult with each other at this stage so that they don't become too dependent on a partner's advice. Circulate and assist as necessary. If students seem to need or want assistance at this stage, read through parts of completed drafts and encourage them to discuss some of their preliminary evaluation with you.

Step 4

6.8 Ask students to exchange drafts and to read their partner's draft carefully.

6.9 After students have read their partner's draft, ask them to apply the eight post-writing questions in 6.7.

6.11 Ask students to apply the points in the specified sections of either Evaluation Checklist A or B. You may want to focus on other sections as well. Most of the post-writing questions focus on content, and for this reason the sections in Evaluation Checklist A and B on organisation/cohesion have been highlighted at this point.

6.12 Again stress the importance of making detailed written comments, either on their partner's draft of on another piece of paper. If some students would prefer to do this after the discussion, this is acceptable as long as the written comments are made in detail.

6.13 Circulate and monitor the process of discussion. Answer questions and deal with problems, as necessary. To provide additional help, especially to weaker groups, you may want to summarise in plenary the main points that have emerged from their discussions with each other. If there are problems which most students are experiencing, deal with them on the board or overhead projector. As in 6.5, ask students individually how they have evaluated their partner's comments and for what reasons.

 Step 5

6.14 After the peer evaluation has been completed, encourage students to continue to work on their drafts before they rewrite. Circulate and offer guidance with the use of the evaluation checklists and appendices. Sections 5 and 6 of Evaluation Checklist A and Sections 4 and 5 of Evaluation Checklist B provide further guidelines which complement those already used in Steps 3 and 4.

6.15 The final draft will probably be produced as homework, as in previous units, unless you feel that further monitoring is necessary. Collect all the written stages of the students' writing process: brainstorming, plans, first drafts and final drafts.
There are many options for further work with the final drafts. They could be circulated around the class, read and evaluated. One example could be chosen from each class (by the students) to be copied and distributed to all classes. Or the final drafts could simply be marked and returned to each student.